# Britain's Best

100 top sites as chosen by the nation

First published in the United Kingdom in 2007 by
Pavilion Books
10 Southcombe Street
London, W14 0RA

An imprint of Anova Books Company Ltd

Design and layout © Pavilion 2007
Text © Pavilion 2007
Foreword © Alan Titchmarsh 2007

Authors  Jane Eastoe and Anny Kilbourne
Editor  Kate Burkhalter
Proofreader  Naomi Waters
Design  John Round Design
Indexer  Derek Copson

ISBN 978 1 86205 805 7

A CIP catalogue record for this book is available
from the British Library.

10 9 8 7 6 5 4 3 2 1

Reproduction by Rival, London
Printed and bound by Qualibris, France

www.anovabooks.com

All opening times and travel details were correct
at the time of going to print. However, please
check with the relevant website before setting out.

*page 1* Salisbury Cathedral
*page 2* Royal Pavilion
*opposite* HMS Victory

Chapter openers
*p16* Bamburgh Castle
*p66* Blenheim Palace
*p92* Lost Gardens of Heligan
*p116* Woolsthorpe Manor
*p166* Battle Abbey
*p214* Clifton Suspension Bridge

# Contents

# Religious Buildings 164

# Best of the Rest 212

# Foreword by Alan Titchmarsh

We are tremendously lucky in Britain to have such a rich cultural heritage which offers a chance to explore so many national treasures. Throughout the series of *Britain's Best* I've been looking at gardens, but also palaces, castles, stately homes and cathedrals. I love gardens, but I'm also fascinated and inspired by history and architecture, which Britain possesses in seemingly infinite variety. It's been fascinating to get indoors for a change – reacquainting myself with some of my favourite places, and discovering new ones recommended by the viewers of *Britain's Best*.

I'm especially enamoured of the Georgian era, when our sense of line, proportion and elegance seemed to be at its height, so one of my favourite places is Chatsworth in Derbyshire, where the gardens and architecture complement each other in the most beautiful landscape. Then there is Kew Gardens, where I trained – a place that will always be dear to my heart and which still possesses the most varied, valuable and glorious collection of plants I know.

Then there's the home of Winston Churchill at Chartwell in Kent – a place that is still so rich in atmosphere that it seems to resonate with the voice of the grand old man of British politics, and where we are given a privileged glimpse into his private life.

This lavish book is a collection of some of the best historical sites in Britain – a tour of grand palaces, impressive cathedrals, ancient castles and gorgeous gardens. The Best of the Rest covers all those other places of which we are so fond, but which defy categorization, and in the process really demonstrates the diversity of Britain's heritage.

It's important that we value and cherish these gems for ourselves, so that future generations can also delight in their discovery. I'm looking forward to visiting even more of these great places and I hope this book will give everyone cause to get out and explore the wonderful treasures we have in Great Britain.

# Introduction

In 2007 UKTV History determined to find Britain's most beloved historical locations. It commissioned a survey which revealed that many people know more about foreign landmarks than they do their own; believing Hadrian's Wall to be in China and confusing the Lost Gardens of Heligan with the Hanging Gardens of Babylon. During the spring and summer of 2007 *Britain's Best* offered a comprehensive guide to some of the most famous sites, and over one million people voted for their personal favourites.

Britain's best sites contain the most riveting real-life stories of days gone by, a history of our past that cries out to be explored. Every location has its own story. It may be bloody or tragic, a testament to the folly of self importance, a fantasy of profligacy, or an inspirational tale of courage, determination or devoted love. Buildings and their contents reveal lives, personalities, politics, the realities of war and the impact of the economy on the ever-changing needs of the human race.

These historic sites give us a better understanding of our place in the world and what others have done before us. Moreover, their scale and the vision behind them is inspirational: who could fail to be moved by the stunning architecture of York Minster and Blenheim Palace or mesmerised

by the sweeping landscapes of Capability Brown at Chatsworth, or the delicately placed floral colour schemes at Sissinghurst gardens.

How incredible to see Skara Brae, a Neolithic village in Orkney, preserved in sand for centuries and uncovered only after massive storms in 1850 and 1925. Alternatively visit Scone Palace, the ancient seat of the kings and queens of Scotland and the original home of the Stone of Scone. Find out where Henry VIII's coffin burst open or where to see Charles I's hatpin, lost during the Battle of Naseby. Learn how Winston Churchill spent his days at home in Chartwell and discover how the amazing Lost Gardens of Heligan were found.

*opposite* Harlech Castle keep
*above* Linlithgow Palace, West Lothian, Scotland
*right* Levens Hall Gardens, Lake District

Stately homes and palaces such as Chatsworth, Blenheim, Castle Howard, Hardwick Hall and Syon Park are breathtaking in their stately grandeur, from collections of Meissen china or paintings by Turner and Canaletto to the economics, politics and downright scheming that the creation and maintenance of such imposing residences entailed. Scrutinize the reality of the lives of the Brontës or William Wordsworth, and revel in the sumptuous interiors of the Brighton Pavilion.

The cathedrals and abbeys that are scattered across the country are the most awe-inspiring pieces of architecture. They are a testament to faith and mark the lives of the great, the good and the royal. It is possible to visit the tomb of Robert the Bruce, allegedly buried without his heart, at Dunfermline Abbey or that of Admiral Lord Nelson in St Paul's Cathedral. Stand on the steps where Thomas á Becket was murdered in Canterbury Cathedral.

The sheer scale of our historical buildings is astounding; Westminster Abbey took more than 250 years to build. The soaring St Paul's is the fourth cathedral to have stood on the site, its predecessor having been burned down in the Great Fire of London. The Reformation and the Dissolution of the Monasteries desecrated many religious buildings leaving a number of exquisitely beautiful ruins such as Glastonbury and Tintern Abbeys, their picturesque decay halted only by impressive preservation works.

Castles bear witness to our bloodthirsty past, a tribute to man's lust for power and our apparent need to fight for what we perceive as right. There is no modern equivalent to the castle, a defensive structure whose usefulness was extinguished with the invention of the cannon. Alnwick Castle was the home of Henry 'Hotspur' Percy who commanded armies of 10,000 men and who helped depose Richard III. Marvel at Mons Meg, a medieval siege gun at Edinburgh Castle, capable of propelling 150-kilogram stones over great distances.

Then there are other great historical curios; the design challenge of Brunel's Clifton Suspension Bridge, and his nautical marvel the SS *Great Britain*, the technical forerunner of modern shipping. Learn how the code to the German Enigma Machine was broken at Bletchley Park, work now credited with helping Britain win World War II. Ponder on just how those stones reached Stonehenge and why Hadrian built that wall?

The National Trust and English Heritage have helped save and preserve many of our finest buildings and gardens. Ongoing maintenance and restoration programmes ensure that all is secured for future generations. Many sites are still privately owned and families fight to stop great historic homes falling into disrepair.

Here we highlight 100 of the nation's top historical sites; it is our interest and enthusiasm that ensures that Britain's history is preserved.

*opposite* Canterbury Cathedral
*above left* Haddon Hall, Derbyshire
*above right* Hadrian's Wall

# Locator Map

**Castles**
1 Warwick Castle
2 Bodiam Castle
3 Caernarfon Castle
4 Carreg Cennen
5 Conwy Castle
6 Dover Castle
7 Harlech Castle
8 Kenilworth Castle
9 Skipton Castle
10 Tintagel Castle
11 Windsor Castle
12 The Tower of London
13 Bamburgh Castle
14 Alnwick Castle
15 Tamworth Castle
16 Edinburgh Castle
17 Kendal Castle
18 Leeds Castle
19 Rochester Castle
20 Stirling Castle
21 Tattershall Castle
22 Eilean Donan

**Palaces**
23 Chatsworth
24 Hampton Court
25 Linlithgow Palace
26 Blenheim Palace
27 Kensington Palace
28 The Palace of Holyroodhouse
29 The Royal Pavilion
30 Scone Palace
31 Buckingham Palace
32 Falkland Palace

**Gardens**
33 Kew Gardens
34 Levens Hall
35 Sissinghurst Castle Garden
36 Castle Howard
37 Stowe Landscape Gardens
38 Tatton Park

39 Stourhead
40 The Lost Gardens of Heligan
41 Knole Gardens
42 Crathes Castle Gardens

**Historic Houses**
43 Chartwell
44 Anne Hathaway's Cottage
45 Apsley House
46 Skara Brae
47 Burghley House
48 Lanhydrock
49 Cragside
50 Harewood House
51 Dove Cottage
52 Haddon Hall
53 Burns Cottage
54 Down House
55 The Brontë Parsonage
56 Eltham Palace
57 Belton House
58 Woolsthorpe Manor
59 Wilberforce House
60 Sandringham House
61 Erddig
62 Hardwick Hall
63 Syon Park

**Religious Buildings**
64 St David's Cathedral
65 Westminster Abbey
66 Ely Cathedral
67 Fountains Abbey
68 St Paul's Cathedral
69 Liverpool Cathedral
70 Iona Abbey
71 Lincoln Cathedral
72 Lindisfarne
73 Glastonbury Abbey
74 Canterbury Cathedral
75 Temple Church
76 Glasgow Cathedral
77 Salisbury Cathedral

78 Tintern Abbey
79 Durham Cathedral
80 Dunfermline Abbey
81 Coventry Cathedral
82 Stonehenge
83 Battle Abbey
84 York Minster

**Best of the Rest**
85 Hadrian's Wall
86 Sherwood Forest
87 Alton Towers
88 The Cabinet War Rooms and Churchill Museum
89 Clifton Suspension Bridge
90 Portmeirion
91 Bletchley Park
92 Sutton Hoo
93 Sir John Soane's Museum
94 Brewery Arts Centre
95 Oxford Colleges
96 Charles Dickens' Museum
97 ss *Great Britain*
98 The Roman Baths at Bath
99 Cambridge Colleges
100 HMS *Victory*

**Key to Facilities**

 Parking

 Café

 Gift shop

 Guide dogs welcome

 Disabled Access

 Facilities for families with small children

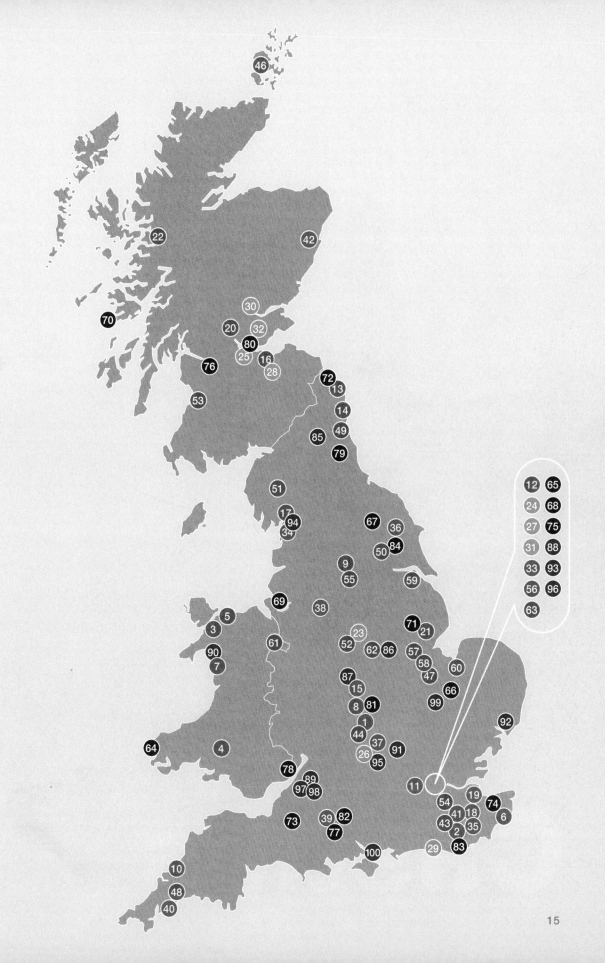

# Castles

# Warwick Castle

Warwick Castle is a building of great beauty, as well as an impressive ancient fortress. It began life as a simple motte-and-bailey castle, but rapidly developed into one of the great medieval strongholds.

There has been a defensive building at Warwick since 914 when King Alfred's daughter, Ethelfleda, ordered the building of an earthen rampart to protect the hilltop settlement of Warwick from Danish invaders. William the Conqueror followed this up with a motte-and-bailey fort in 1068 and in 1260 the castle was reconstructed from stone.

William de Beaufort inherited the castle from his uncle in 1268 and a dynasty was founded that would last 148 years and witness much treachery and bloodshed. During this time the castle was continually extended; Caesar's Tower and the dungeons were constructed in 1350 and the thirty-nine-metre tall Guy's Tower was built in 1395. Fortifications were added by Richard III until his untimely death at the Battle of Bosworth in 1485, which accounts for the reduced stature of the Bear and Clarence Towers originally intended to equal Guy's Tower in height.

The title of Earl of Warwick seems to have been a poisoned chalice; Richard Neville, who was made Earl of Warwick in 1449, helped to depose both Henry VI and Edward IV during the Wars of the Roses, earning himself the epithet of 'the Kingmaker'. The interfering and manipulative Neville was finally defeated at the Battle of Barnet in 1471. King Edward IV then gave his brother the title of Earl of Warwick and followed up by appointing his nephew, but proceeded to execute both.

The castle has played host to many kings and queens including Queen Elizabeth I, King William III, Queen Victoria and Queen Elizabeth II. It remained home to the Earls of Warwick until 1978 when it was purchased by the Tussaud's Group. Extensive restoration work was undertaken and elaborate reconstructions of castle life have been created, including that deadly military machine the trebuchet. It stands eighteen metres tall, weighs twenty-two tonnes and is regularly fired. The eight restored state rooms house an impressive collection of antiques.

*opposite and overleaf* Views of the medieval Warwick Castle.

**Warwick Castle**
**Warwick**
**CV34 4QU**

**Tel 0870 442 2000**
**www.warwick-castle.co.uk**

**Opening**
Open daily except Christmas Day. Disabled access is limited: please check the website.

**Getting There**
Warwick Castle is 8 miles east of Stratford-upon-Avon and is 2 miles from junction 15 of the M40. Warwick railway station is 1 mile from the castle; trains run from London Marylebone and Birmingham Snow Hill.

**Concessions**
Children 4–17 years; under 4s free
Families
Over 60s
Students

**Facilities**

## INTERESTING FACT
In 1431 Richard de Beauchamp, thirteenth Earl of Warwick, supervised both Joan of Arc's trial for heresy and her subsequent burning in Rouen, France.

# Bodiam Castle

By the early 1370s, England was faring badly in the Hundred Years War, losing control of the Channel. French pirates were active along the English coast. In 1377, two Cinque Ports – Rye and Winchelsea – were destroyed. Sir Edward Dalyngrigge was then sent to survey Winchelsea and in 1385 he asked Richard II for permission to fortify his own manor, ten miles inland.

Rather than improve the existing property, Dalyngrigge started work on a new site, in a strategic position overlooking the river Rother. His fortification at Bodiam

was one of the last to be built before the development of siege artillery changed their design for ever. It is many peoples' idea of the perfect medieval castle, with towered walls rising out of a broad, spring-fed moat. Three bridges over two islands connect to the gateway.

Bodiam was also a grand home and status symbol. The interior is now in ruins, but there are plenty of clues to the preoccupations of its inhabitants. There is a great hall surrounded by a buttery, pantry and kitchen and personal quarters for Dalyngrigge and his wife. Traceried windows, numerous fireplaces and a chapel also indicate that the castle was not purely a battle station.

After Dalyngrygge, Bodiam Castle passed to other Sussex families, but gradually decayed, before being restored by Lord Curzon in 1905.

**Near Robertsbridge
East Sussex
TN32 5UA**

**Tel 01580 830436
www.nationaltrust.org.uk**

**Opening**
Bodiam is open daily from the beginning of March to the end of October and then at weekends until February 2008.

**Getting There**
3 miles south of Hawkhurst. Trains to Wadhurst (12 miles) and Robertsbridge (5 miles, but no bus link). Stagecoach bus 309, Hawkhurst – Hastings. Bodiam can also be visited by ferry, from Newenden Bridge on the A28.

**Concessions**
Children 5–16 years
Families
Pre-booked groups

**Facilities**

# Caernarfon Castle

The castle at Caernarfon was raised not only as a fortification, or even a royal residence, but also as a dramatic symbol of English dominion over the Welsh. Its position, at the mouth of the river Seiont and overlooking the Menai Straits, was both defensively and commercially ideal.

In 1283, Edward I finally defeated the last of the Welsh princes who had opposed his rule. To consolidate his position, Edward took over the site of an earlier Norman castle – which had in turn been a Roman fort – and started work on a huge edifice whose unusual design incorporating polygonal towers and coloured bands of stone, echoed the fortresses of Rome and Constantinople. The outer curtain wall contains a warren of passages at two different levels, nine towers and two gatehouses. The King's Gate, although it was never completed, forces any attacker to pass two drawbridges, five doors and six portcullises, all overlooked by arrow holes. Despite its protection,

**Castle Ditch**
**Caernarfon**
**Gwynedd**
**LL5 2AY**

**Tel 01286 677617**
**www.cadw.wales.gov.uk**

**Opening**
Open daily, all year round.

**Getting there**
Caernarfon is 16 miles from Bangor. Buses from Bangor.

**Concessions**
Children 5–16 years
Disabled (carers free)
Pre-booked groups

**Facilities**

the castle was overrun by Welsh rebels in 1293; having overcome this rebellion, Edward responded by intensifying the building work. The castle as we see it today was largely complete by 1330.

As a further gesture of English domination, Edward ensured that his son, Edward of Caernarfon, was born in the castle. And it was also here that, in 1301, the seventeen-year-old was invested as the first Prince of Wales.

Caernarfon remained the effective capital of north Wales for two centuries. But in 1485 Henry Tudor

came to the English throne. He was of Welsh origin, and with his accession, relations between the two countries improved. Heavy fortifications in Wales were no longer needed and Caernarfon was one of several impressive castles that were allowed to fall into ruin. It was extensively restored in the late nineteenth century and in 1969 saw the investiture of the current Prince of Wales.

*above Caernarfon Harbour and Castle.*

# Carreg Cennen

Carreg Cennen occupies one of the most dramatic spots of all British castles, on the crest of a 300-foot limestone crag. It was possibly an Iron Age hillfort; archaeological evidence, including human remains, shows that there was habitation on the site well before the Romans. But the medieval castle probably started life in the late twelfth century. It was built by the Welsh Deheubarth family and the first recorded mention of Carreg Cennen occurs in 1248, when the mother of Rhys Fychan, a Deheubarth descendant, handed the castle to the English to spite her son; but he was able to recapture it before the English could take possession. For nearly thirty years, Carreg Cennen changed hands between Rhys and his uncle, and between the Welsh and the English.

In 1277, the castle was captured by the English king Edward I, who gave it to one of his barons, John Giffard; he had commanded the English troops at the final defeat of the Welsh princes at Cilmeri. It was probably John Giffard who remodelled the castle into the form we see today.

The castle's relatively simple layout is perfectly adapted to the rock on which it stands. There is a square inner ward and an outer ward guarding the north and east sides, which do not have the natural protection of the cliff. There is also a very well-protected gatehouse.

After John Gifford and his son, the castle's owners included John of Gaunt and Henry Bolingbroke (the future Henry IV). During Owain Glyndwr's revolt at the start of the fifteenth century, the castle was damaged but never captured. Subsequent repairs were short-lived. During the Wars of the Roses, Carreg Cennen was a Lancastrian stronghold. Shortly after the Yorkist victory at the Battle of Mortimer's Cross in 1461, the Lancastrians holding the castle were forced to surrender. Hundreds of Yorkist soldiers set about demolishing the fortress and it has been a ruin ever since.

*opposite Spectacular view of Carreg Cennen castle with the Carmarthenshire coutryside in the background.*

**Carreg Cennen**
**Trapp**
**Llandeilo**
**Carmarthen, SA19 6TS**

**Tel 01558 822291**
**www.carregcennen.co.uk**

**Opening**
The castle is open daily, except 24–26 December and New Years Day.

**Getting There**
4.5 miles south-east of Llandeilo. Buses from Llandovery and Carmarthen to Llandeilo. Trains from Shrewsbury and Swansea call at Llandeilo.

**Concessions**
Children
Families
Groups

**Facilities**

---

**SPECIAL FEATURE**
Steep steps in the south-east corner of the site lead to a cave under the castle. It is likely that the cave would have been walled up to prevent its use by attackers.

# Conwy Castle

Conwy is one of the castles built by Edward I to consolidate his position in Wales after the defeat of the Welsh princes in the early 1280s. It was largely completed in a very short space of time – around four years – which is all the more remarkable since the castle and town were raised as one unit, within an outer wall.

The work was supervised by the celebrated architect James of St George, brought from his native Savoy by the king. Its estimated that when the building work was fully underway, some 1500 men were employed. That the king was willing to make such a huge investment is an illustration of the importance given to the security of north Wales.

But within just fifty years, the slate roofs were proving insufficient to keep out the harsh weather.

**Conwy Castle**
**Conwy, LL32 8AY**

**Tel 01492 592358**
**www.cadw.wales.gov.uk**

**Opening**
Conwy Castle is open daily throughout the year, with the exception of 24–26 December and New Years Day.

**Getting There**
Conway is on the A55. Trains call at Llandudno Junction, approximately a mile and a half from the castle. There are buses from Bangor, Llandudno and Caernarfon.

**Concessions**
Children under 15 years
Disabled and carers
Families
Groups

**Facilities**

They leaked, and the wooden structures underneath started to decay. In 1346, the substitution of the lead roofs began. To carry their weight, fifteen huge stone arches were erected in the great hall buildings and royal apartments – although only two survive today.

Decay continued to plague Conwy's custodians as the years passed, until, in 1627, the castle was sold for £100 to Charles I's Secretary of State, who became Lord Conway and Killultagh. It was hoped that his family would repair and maintain the buildings, but the start of the Civil War ended those hopes. It happened that John Williams, the archbishop of York, was a Conwy man. He duly returned home and fortified and garrisoned the castle for the king at his own expense, although he was eventually forced to side with the besieging parliamentary forces to save the town from destruction.

After the Civil War, the castle was returned to the Conwy family, but the cost of its upkeep was prohibitive and it was gradually dismantled. It was not until the nineteenth century that efforts were made to preserve the monument and provision was made for visitors.

*opposite Conwy Castle from the harbour.*

# Dover Castle

The location of Dover Castle is as significant as the buildings themselves. It sits on top of the White Cliffs, looking out over the narrowest section of the Channel, with France only 26 miles away. There have been fortifications on the site since the Iron Age. The Romans occupied the site and built a lighthouse, which can still be seen. Dover, one of the Cinque Ports, was central to William I's coastal defences. But the castle as it now stands is a largely Norman construction.

Henry II established the core of the castle during the 1180s. It was centred on a massive keep and two concentric towered walls. In 1216, a group of rebel nobles invited Louis VIII of France to usurp the Engish throne. Louis' forces besieged Dover and had some success in penetrating the outer walls but failed to capture the castle itself. The siege led to an expansion of the castle by Henry III, who added a massive, towered, outer curtain wall, stretching right to the edges of the cliffs. The castle's narrow escape was also the impetus to extend a medieval network of tunnels in the rock under the castle, in order to provide an extra line of defence.

After his excommunication by the Pope and a peace treaty between France and Spain, Henry VIII's nervousness about an invasion of England led him to build a line of coastal defences and add to the fortifications at Dover. During the Civil War, while many historical buildings were severely damaged or destroyed, the castle survived undamaged, after a night-time raid by a handful of Dover townsfolk with Parliamentarian loyalties took the Royalist garrison by surprise. Dover Castle went on to become an important defence in the Napoleonic wars, and during the Second World War it served as the command centre for Operation Dynamo – the evacuation of Allied troops from northern France.

*opposite* Dover Castle in Kent.

**Dover Castle
Kent
CT16 1HU**

Tel 01304 211067
www.english-heritage.org.uk

**Opening**
Dover Castle is open daily in summer, and from Thursday to Monday, November to January. It is closed from 24 – 26 December, and on New Year's Day.

**Getting There**
The castle is to the east of Dover town centre. Trains run to Dover Priory (1.5 miles) and there are buses from Dover town centre and local areas.

**Concessions**
Children 5–16 years
Families
Over-60s
Students with ID
Unemployed

**Facilities**

> **INTERESTING FACT**
> The tunnels under the castle have been used variously as a barracks housing two thousand men, air-raid shelter, a telegraph exchange and a naval command centre.

# Harlech Castle

Harlech was one of a group of fourteen imposing new castles built for King Edward I in the last quarter of the thirteenth century. The aim was to consolidate the king's position in Wales, after the defeat and death of the last Welsh Prince of all Wales, Llewelyn ap Gruffudd, near Builth in 1282.

As soon as Edward's forces reached Harlech, work began on the castle. £100 in cash was sent under heavy guard to commence the work and three years later, in the summer of 1286, nearly 950 men are recorded as being employed on the site. Thanks to Edward's family connections with Savoy, the work was directed by James of St George, a celebrated Savoyard master-mason and military engineer.

**Harlech Castle**
**Harlech**
**Gwynedd**
**LL46 2YH**

**Tel 01766 780552**
**www.cadw.wales.gov.uk**

**Opening**
The castle is open daily throughout the year, except 24–26 December and New Years Day. Times are available from the website.

**Getting There**
Harlech station is within a short walking distance of the castle. Trains run from Shrewsbury and Machynlleth/Pwllheli.

**Concessions**
Children under 15 years
Disabled and carers
Families
Pre-booked groups (15 or more)

**Facilities**

His influence can be seen particularly in the rounded arches of the castle, and in the window design in the gatehouse, where James probably lived during construction. Astonishingly, the castle was finished and garrisoned within six years.

The castle was put to the test very quickly, when it was attacked during the rising of the Welsh princes in 1294. The garrison was able to hold out because of the vital access the castle gave to the sea, which allowed Harlech to receive supplies from Ireland. Despite Harlech's strength, it was seized by Owain Glyndwr in the first years of the fifteenth century and

remained in Welsh hands until its recapture by Prince Harry of Monmouth – later to become Henry V.

The song 'Men of Harlech' is traditionally supposed to have been created during the Wars of the Roses, when the castle was held for the Lancastrians and besieged by the Yorkists, who were able to gain control of the castle in less than a month.

In the Civil War, Harlech was the last royalist stronghold to fall to the parliamentarians. Its defeat marked the end of the war. Since then, Harlech Castle has remained undisturbed on its often-painted crag against the backdrop of Snowdonia.

## SPECIAL FEATURE
The path from the sea gate to the castle has always been vulnerable. In the 1290s, the vital 'way from the sea' was enclosed with a wall and a new tower.

*above* *Harlech Castle, with Mount Snowdon in the background.*

# Kenilworth Castle

There have been fortifications of some sort on the site of Kenilworth Castle since well before Norman times. But in 1122, Geoffrey de Clinton, Henry I's chamberlain, built a Norman motte-and-bailey, a simple wooden tower within a circular enclosure. By the end of the twelfth century, it had been rebuilt in stone. Probably regarded as too strong to be left in private hands, the castle was taken over by the crown. The towered curtain wall was added by King John, who also built a fortified dam that created a large lake, making Kenilworth a virtual island fortress.

The castle remained in royal hands until it came into the possession of Simon de Montfort in 1244. De Montfort, despite being the brother-in-law of Henry III, rebelled against what he saw as the excessive power of the king. With a group of supportive barons, he took refuge in the castle in 1266 – they were able to hold out for nine months, until hunger and disease defeated them.

In 1389, John of Gaunt, Duke of Lancaster, began remodelling the Great Hall and state rooms of the inner court, transforming Kenilworth from a fortification into a palace. Further developments were made under

**Kenilworth**
**Warwickshire**
**CV8 1NE**

**Tel 01926 864152**
**www.english-heritage.org.uk/kenilworth**

**Opening**
Castle open daily throughout year.
Closed 24 – 26 December and New Year's Day.

**Getting There**
Clearly signposted from Kenilworth town centre. Both Warwick and Coventry are 5 miles away. Buses run from both towns, and from Leamington Spa.

**Concessions**
Children under 16
Families
Over-60s
Pre-booked groups
Students
Unemployed

**Facilities**

*opposite The ruins of Kenilworth Castle.*

**SPECIAL FEATURE**
The keep was the first section of the castle to be built and it became the defensive centre of the complex. In 1266 it withstood the longest siege of medieval times.

of the entertainments laid on by Robert Dudley, Earl of Leicester, for Elizabeth I in 1575. As custodian, his extensive improvements included an entire suite specially for the queen, who visited three times. One party in 1575 famously lasted for nineteen days.

After being allowed to fall into ruin, Kenilworth became the property of the nation in 1938.

Henry V, who built a pavilion – the Pleasaunce – at the end of the lake. It was here that, according to tradition, Henry received the insulting 'gift' of tennis balls from the French, an incident which led to the Agincourt campaign. The Pleasaunce came to be a focal point

# Skipton Castle

The first castle at Skipton was built shortly after 1090, in defence against incursions by the Scots. It was an earth and timber construction, typical of its time. But in 1310, Robert Clifford was appointed first Lord of Skipton and the castle came into his hands. He began a complete reconstruction in stone. When Robert was killed at Bannockburn in 1314 the rebuilding work was taken over by his son, Roger.

The twin-towered gatehouse is a remnant from the fourteenth-century outer defences. There are still grooves for the portcullis and an opening in the masonry for the drawbar of the great door. Beyond the gatehouse is the outer bailey, surrounded by a light curtain wall. The inner bailey is surrounded by a wall with six towers, constructed in a D-shape facing away from the 100-foot cliffs immediately below to the north. These walls contain a courtyard, the Conduit Court, which is surrounded by Tudor domestic buildings. Water would have been brought into the castle in elmwood pipes, but there was also provision for times of siege when rainwater could be collected on the roof, then stored in a cistern under the Conduit Court.

This measure came into its own during the Civil War, when Sir John Mallory held the castle for the royalists. A parliamentarian siege lasted for three years, before Mallory and his 300 men surrendered in 1645. Oliver Cromwell saw the castle as such a threat to the security of the north that he ordered it to be 'slighted', or rendered indefensible. When Lady Anne Clifford was granted permission to carry out restoration twelve years later, it was on condition that it never be returned to 'fighting condition'; walls had to be made thinner, and ceilings too weak to support cannon. The yew tree in the Conduit Court was planted in 1659, and the inscription over the main entrance commemorates the completion of Anne Clifford's restoration.

*opposite Skipton Castle, north Yorkshire.*

## SPECIAL FEATURE

Masons' marks can be seen in the stonework of the main entrance. These personalised marks by the craftsmen identified their work, so they could be paid.

**Skipton Castle
North Yorkshire
BD23 1AW**

**Tel 01756 792442
www.skiptoncastle.co.uk**

**Opening**
The castle is open daily, with the exception of 25 December.

**Getting There**
The castle is in Skipton town centre, at the top end of the High Street. The town is easily accessible by road and there is a car park off the High Street. There is a direct train service from London King's Cross to Skipton; trains also run from Leeds and Bradford.

**Concessions**
Children 5–17 years; under 5s free
Families (2 adults, up to 3 children)
Over 60
Students

**Facilities**

# Tintagel Castle

Tintagel Castle sits on one of the most romantic and dramatic stretches of British coastline; high on top of a neck of land that joins Tintagel Island to the mainland. According to legend Uther Pendragon and his son King Arthur lived here, while below the castle is Merlin's cave.

Archaeological evidence shows that Tintagel once housed a Roman settlement and military outpost. Digs have also found evidence of fifth and sixth-century settlements and the quantity of imported luxury goods indicate that this must have been the home of the kings of Dumnonia, a kingdom comprising Cornwall,

**Tintagel Castle**
**Tintagel**
**Cornwall**
**PL34 OHE**

**Tel 01840 770328**
**www.english-heritage.org.uk**

**Opening**
Open daily, except 24–26 December and New Year's Day. Disabled access is limited; please see the website for further information.

**Getting There**
The castle is on the neck of Tintagel Head; access is via 100 steep steps. The bus service is limited – number 524 Bude to Wadebridge, via Tintagel or number 594 Bude to Truro via Tintagel (the 555 connects at Wadebridge to Bodmin Parkway, the nearest train station).

**Concessions**
Children 5–15 years; under 5s free
Over 60s
Students, Unemployed

**Facilities**

> **INTERESTING FACT**
> Legend has it that King Mark resided at Tintagel. His nephew Tristan fell in love with Mark's queen, Yseult (Isolde) and their doomed romance was played out here.

Devon and parts of Somerset. It was during this time that a large defensive ditch was built, effectively cutting off access to the headland and giving the area its name; Din Tagell – the Fort of the Constriction.

In 1136 Geoffrey of Monmouth wrote in his *History of the Kings of Britain* that King Arthur had been conceived at Tintagel; other later tales told of his birth and life there. There is however no direct evidence to connect Arthur to Tintagel.

When the Normans reached Cornwall they heard that the ancient seat of Cornish kings was located on top of Tintagel's headland, battered on three sides by the unforgiving Atlantic. Around 1233 Earl Richard of Cornwall, younger brother of Henry III, decided that this would be an appropriate place to build his castle, although it would serve no real strategic or defensive purpose. Tintagel is said to be England's earliest linear castle.

Fortifications are in two sections, on the landward side the upper and lower wards stand on the edge of a sheer cliff face, while the inner ward is on a narrow ridge leading to the small island. The castle was originally joined by a causeway, but erosion has virtually destroyed it and access is now gained by two steep stairways. Later earls of Cornwall made little use of the castle and it fell into ruin as early as the late fifteenth century. Although in ruins, the amazing scenery and dramatic atmosphere make this a truly spectacular place to visit.

*opposite A dramatic view from Tintagel Castle.*

# Windsor Castle

Windsor Castle is the oldest continuously inhabited castle in the world. William I built a wooden fortress on the site to guard the western approaches to London. It was replaced in stone by Henry II in the 1170s.

Over the centuries, the castle has been extended, improved and adapted to suit different ages. Edward III, who was born at the castle, spent decades remodelling it. In the 1390s, under Richard II, restoration was undertaken on the old St George's Chapel. The clerk of the works was Geoffrey Chaucer.

Efforts were made through the centuries to make the castle less of a fortress and more of a palace, but Edward VI thought that the lack of gardens and galleries still made it feel like a prison. This has been remedied since, firstly by his sister, Elizabeth I, who built the North Terrace as a pleasant covered walk.

The parliamentatrians captured the castle in the Civil War, but after his Restoration, Charles II made Windsor even more splendid. Later George IV re-introduced a Gothic style to match the medieval sections.

Ten monarchs are buried at Windsor, among them Charles I, whose body had to be smuggled in at night.

**Windsor Castle**
**Windsor, SL4 1LJ**

**Tel 020 7766 7304 (Royal Collection Information)**
**www.royalcollection.org.uk**

**Opening**
Windsor Castle is open daily throughout the year, with the exception of 25–26 December and 18 June. The State Apartments are closed on 16, 17 and 19 June.

**Getting There**
Trains run to Windsor Central from London Paddington or Waterloo. There are also buses from London.

**Concessions**
Children 5–17 years; under 5s free
Families (2 adults, 3 children)
Over 60s
Students

**Facilities**

**SPECIAL FEATURE**
The present St George's Chapel was begun by Edward IV and finished by Henry VIII, and is one of the finest examples of late medieval architecture in Europe.

*opposite* The Queen's residence, Windsor Castle.

# The Tower of London

**The Tower of London was begun in its present form by William the Conqueror, who desired both a fortification and a royal palace.**

Although the White – or Great – Tower is the typical iconic image, the Tower of London is in fact several buildings, set within two rings of defensive walls and a moat. After its foundation, various monarchs extended and developed the Tower, which continued to be a royal home until Oliver Cromwell demolished the old palatial buildings.

Besides housing monarchs, the Tower has been a prison, a place of execution, a museum, a safe store for the Crown Jewels, and a zoo. As a prison, it was reserved for those of high rank and religious dissidents. Those held there included Elizabeth I, Walter Raleigh – who was allowed to move his wife and children in with him and grow tobacco on Tower Green – and even the Kray twins, who were imprisoned for failing to report for national service in 1932.

Executions generally took place in public, on Tower Hill, but some were held privately on Tower Green. Henry VIII's wives Anne Boleyn and Catherine Howard were granted that privilege.

There have been at least six ravens recorded as resident at the Tower from its first days. The legend that their removal would lead to the downfall of the kingdom is thought to date back to the reign of Charles II. During his reign, the Astronomer Royal complained about the birds. But Charles was so alarmed by the probably newly invented tale – and so insecure as the newly-restored monarch – that the ravens stayed, and the Royal Observatory moved to Greenwich.

For centuries the Tower also housed a small zoo or menagerie, started in 1235 with the gift to Henry III of three lions. It endured until the last animals were moved to London Zoo, in 1835.

*opposite The Tower of London.*

**The Tower of London
EC3N 4AB**

**Tel 020 7709 0765
Tel 0870 756 7070 (bookings)
www.tower-of-london.org.uk**

**Opening**
Open daily throughout the year, except 25 and 26 December and New Year's Day.

**Getting There**
The Tower is on the River Thames, near London Bridge. The nearest Underground station is Tower Hill. Numerous buses from other parts of London.

**Concessions**
Children 5–16 years; under 5s free
Disabled
Families
Over 60s
Students

**Facilities**

**INTERESTING FACT**
The Crown Jewels have been kept at the Tower since 1303. In 1671, an attempt to steal them was foiled, and the Jewels have been kept under armed guard ever since.

# Bamburgh Castle

**This magnificent coastal castle is set in the most ravishing windswept scenery. It has a rich and turbulent history dating back many centuries.**

In the sixth century the native Britons were struggling to defend themselves against the invading Saxons and Angles. In AD 547 King Ida the Flamebearer landed an expeditionary force at Flamborough Head and conquered Northumberland. Their largest settlement was named Bebbanburgh after Bebba, the wife of King Ida's grandson. However it was not until the Norman conquest that the castle we see today began to take shape. The formidable castle the Normans built stood until the end of the Wars of the Roses; it was besieged many times but never taken. After the invention of the canon however,

castles were no longer impregnable and therefore of little value.

Bamburgh Castle and its surrounding lands belonged to the Crown and during the latter part of the reign of Elizabeth I she gave the castle to Claudius Forster. His son Tom Forster took part in the first Jacobite rebellion in 1715. Tom had joined the rebels in the hope of improving his financial and personal standing and they made him a general. Once on the battlefield however, he took one look at the enemy and surrendered. He was taken to Newgate prison and incarcerated, but eventually managed to escape, dressed as a maid, with the help of his sister Dorothy.

The Forster family were soon bankrupt and sold their lands to Lord Crewe, Bishop of Durham. He set out to assist the poor of the parish and also devised a system of signals between the castle and Holy Island (see pages 184-185) to help protect seamen along the treacherous coast. Massive chains were used to help pull stranded ships to shore and these are on display in the castle.

The castle was sold again at the end of the nineteenth century to Lord Armstrong, engineer and industrialist, who restored it at a cost of £1 million; the castle today remains in the ownership of the Armstrong family. It houses collections of china, porcelain, paintings, furniture, arms and armour.

*opposite Bamburgh Castle on the rugged Northumberland coast.*

**Bamburgh Castle**
**Bamburgh**
**Northumberland**
**NE69 7DF**

**Tel 01668 214515**
**www.bamburghcastle.com**

**Opening**
Open daily March – October. Disabled access is limited; please check the website.

**Getting There**
Bamburgh Castle is situated 42 miles north of Newcastle-upon-Tyne, 20 miles south of Berwick-upon-Tweed and 6 miles east of Belford on the B1342. There is a limited local bus service.

**Concessions**
Children 6–15 years; under 6s free
Over 60s

**Facilities**

# Alnwick Castle

Alnwick Castle has been home to the Percys, earls and dukes of Northumberland, since 1309. The earliest mention of the castle in the history books dates from 1096 when Yves de Vescy became Baron of Alnwick and built the earliest parts of the castle.

The castle was first restored as far back as the early 1300s by the First Lord Percy of Alnwick and parts of this restoration remain, including the Abbott's Tower, the Middle Gateway and the Constable's Tower.

The Percys became one of the most powerful families in England. The infamous Sir Henry 'Hotspur' Percy, 1364–1403, commanded armies of up to 10,000 men in battles against the Scots; he was finally kidnapped and held to ransom. He had a hand in deposing Richard II and helping Henry IV to get the throne. He was finally killed in the Battle of Shrewsbury in 1403 rebelling against Henry IV. The ninth earl was implicated in the Gunpowder Plot and imprisoned in the Tower of London for seventeen years, though in fact it was his distant cousin and servant, Thomas Percy who was one of the principal plotters and who was shot trying to escape.

In 1766 the first Duke of Northumberland hired Capability Brown to transform the landscape, and James Paine and celebrated architect Robert Adam to transform the castle into a palace in the gothic style. The fourth Duke travelled widely and explored Egypt: many of his finds can be seen in the castle museum. He also ensured that the interior of the castle was again refurbished, this time in the Italian Renaissance style, working with eminent architects Anthony Salvin and Luigi Canina.

More recently a twelve-acre contemporary garden comprising a series of busy and tranquil spaces was opened in 2002 with spectacular water displays and one of the largest tree houses in the world.

Alnwick Castle is the second largest inhabited castle in England, the first being Windsor Castle (see pages 40-41). It featured as Hogwarts in the first two *Harry Potter* films and is littered with historical imprints of the colourful family who have lived there.

*opposite Sunset at Alnwick Castle, Northumberland.*

Alnwick Castle
Alnwick
Northumberland
NE66 1NQ

Tel 01665 510777
www.alnwickcastle.com

**Opening**
Open daily April – October; for further details please check the website. Disabled access is limited; please contact the castle for more information.

**Getting There**
Alnwick Castle is situated 33 miles north of Newcastle-upon-Tyne and 80 miles south of Edinburgh. The nearest train station is Alnmouth, 4 miles from Alnwick. Bus 518 runs from here to the castle.

**Concessions**
Children 5–14 years; under 5s free
Families, Over 60s, Students

**Facilities**

**INTERESTING FACT**
Fearless Harry Hotspur was born in the gatehouse. His heroics, aged just fourteen, at the siege of Berwick earned him his nickname.

# Tamworth Castle

The oldest part of Tamworth Castle was built just after the Norman Conquest. Over the centuries five rich and powerful families made it their home, each making their mark, with the last leaving in 1897. It has withstood sieges and surrendered to parliamentarian forces in the English Civil War.

The Normans are responsible for the original motte-and-bailey castle that was built between 1070 and 1080. Later in the twelfth century one Robert Marmion crowned the motte with a polygonal shell keep and protected its gate with a small square flanking tower.

Built around the medieval banqueting hall and courtyard is an assortment of Tudor and Jacobean buildings. A huge curtain wall in herringbone masonry leads from the keep to a twin towered gatehouse that was built in the thirteenth century. Fifteen rooms are open to visitors including the magnificent Great Hall, dungeon and a Victorian suite of rooms that includes a bedroom, bathroom and breakfast parlour. Royal visitors have included Henry II, King James I and his son Prince Charles. Tamworth Castle was twice threatened with destruction, once by King John in 1215 and once by Oliver Cromwell in 1645.

Legend has it that a black lady haunts the Lady's Chamber. She is reputed to be a ninth-century nun named Editha who was expelled with her sisters from Polesworth Abbey by the first Baron Marmion. The continued prayers of the homeless nuns summoned her from her grave and in 1139 the third baron, saw a vision of her in his bedchamber. She told him that if the nuns were not returned to the abbey he would suffer an untimely death, then she struck him. He was badly injured and suffered considerable pain. His friends advised him to return the nuns to the abbey and his pain only stopped when he vowed to do so.

The castle was put up for auction in the late 1890s and Tamworth Corporation purchased it for £3,000 to celebrate Queen Victoria's Diamond Jubilee in 1897. The castle is set in a very beautiful park with floral terraces; it also has a sensory garden.

*opposite Tamworth Castle.*

---

Tamworth Castle
The Holloway
Ladybank
Tamworth
Staffordshire
B79 7NA

Tel 01827 709626
**www.tamworthcastle.co.uk**

**Opening**
Open Tuesday – Sunday from April – October. For further dates please check the website. Disabled access is limited.

**Getting There**
The castle is situated in the heart of Tamworth. By car it is a 20-minute drive from Birmingham. Trains run from Birmingham to Tamworth regularly; the castle is a 10-minute walk from the station. Local buses run frequently.

**Concessions**
Children 6–16 years; under 6s free
Families
Over 60s
Students

**Facilities**

---

**SPECIAL FEATURE**
Walk the castle parapet from where the White Lady plunged to her death after her lover, Sir Tarquin, was slain in combat by Sir Lancelot.

# Edinburgh Castle

Edinburgh Castle is a great Scottish icon looming high over the city on an 80-metre-high plug of volcanic rock, overlooking one of Europe's great capital cities.

For centuries it was a favourite residence of Scottish kings and queens and witnessed some of the greatest – and darkest – events in the nation's history.

The castle is a major piece of defensive work that was tested by attack or siege on no less than thirteen occasions. It was built during the reign of David I in 1124 and further developed by the Stuarts. The oldest part of the fortress is Queen Margaret's Chapel, built by David I in memory of his mother.

The castle has borne witness to many historical events, births and deaths alike. In 1440 the teenage earl William Douglas and his younger brother were invited for a sumptuous banquet with the ten-year-old King James II. The Douglas family were feared rivals for the crown and at the end of the meal the two boys were presented with the head of a black bull – a sure sign of death – before being dragged away for execution.

In Mary's room you can see the tiny cell where Mary Queen of Scots gave birth to the son who grew up to unite the crowns of Scotland and England as King James VI and I.

The castle is home to the Honours of Scotland – the Scottish crown jewels – and to curiosities such as Mons Meg, a great medieval siege gun capable of firing 150kg stones as far as 3.2km and last in use in 1681. A more recent attraction is the Prisons of War exhibit, which shows the vaults as they were at the end of the 18th century. Visitors can also see the royal apartments, the great hall, the national war memorial and three military museums.

> **INTERESTING FACT**
> The Stone of Destiny, the coronation seat of Scottish kings, resides in Edinburgh Castle. Stolen in 1296, it was kept in Westminster Abbey until its return in 1996.

**Edinburgh Castle
Castle Hill
Edinburgh
EH1 2NG**

**Tel 0131 225 9846
www.historic-scotland.gov.uk**

**Opening**
Daily except for Christmas Day and Boxing Day.

**Getting There**
Travel to Edinburgh by air, road, train or coach. The castle looms over the city skyline and is impossible to miss.

**Concessions**
Children 5–15 years; under 5s free
Over 60s
Unemployed

**Facilities**

*opposite Edinburgh Castle from the fountain in Princes Street Gardens.*
*overleaf Edinburgh Castle.*

# Kendal Castle

**Kendal Castle is a beautiful ruin, believed to be the birthplace of Katherine Parr, the sixth wife of Henry VIII. It sits in a commanding position above Kendal with stunning views in all directions.**

The castle was originally constructed of earth and timber but was rebuilt in stone in the late twelfth century. It was home to the barons of Kendal, of which the Parr family were the best known.

Kendal Castle was originally a motte-and-bailey design, made of limestone and slate. It sits on a hill known as a drumlin: a mass of gravel and clay left by a glacier in the last Ice Age. Over the centuries the soil on the hill has been washed away so that the foundations are now two to three feet above ground. It once had six towers and fourteen-foot-high outer walls. Parts of the walls and towers remain however and there is an impressive vaulted undercroft.

The last of the Parr family to own the castle was Katherine's brother, William who supported Lady Jane Grey's attempt on the throne; he was stripped of his baronetcy in 1555 and the bailiffs were sent in, sealing Kendal Castle's fate. The castle was in a ruinous state by 1572. In 1581 Elizabeth I gave the castle to the Earl of Warwick but it continued to decline with successive owners. At one point in it was even used as a quarry.

**Kendal Castle**
**Castle Hill**
**Kendal**
**Cumbria**
**LA9 7BL**

**www.kendalmuseum.org.uk**

**Opening**
Open daily

**Getting There**
Kendal Castle is 24 miles north of Lancaster and is located west of the town centre on a high ridge.

**Concessions**
Free entry

**Facilities**

In 1897 Kendal Corporation bought Castle Hill for the public to celebrate Queen Victoria's Diamond Jubilee. Kendal Museum houses a permanent exhibition on the life of the castle, its occupants and the town below.

*below Amongst the ruins of Kendal Castle.*

### SPECIAL FEATURE
The original key to the castle can still be seen in the nearby Kendal Museum; it is made of cast iron, is ten inches long and weighs four pounds.

# Leeds Castle

Leeds Castle was built in 1194, on two islands in a lake, by Robert de Crevecoeur, the descendant of one of William the Conqueror's lords. It acquired its name because it is adjacent to the village of Leeds near Maidstone.

The castle passed into royal hands in 1278 and became part of the English Queen's Dower – the settlement widowed queens receive on the death of their husbands. It was held by six medieval queens including Eleanor of Castille, Margaret of France, Isabella of France, Joan of Navarre, Anne of Bohemia and Catherine de Valois.

Henry VIII was a frequent visitor, but his son, Edward VI, granted the castle to one of Henry's

**Leeds Castle**
**Maidstone**
**Kent**
**ME17 1PL**

**Tel 01622 765400**
**www.leeds-castle.com**

**Opening**
Open daily except for 3 and 4 November and Christmas Day. For 2008 dates please check website.

**Getting There**
Leeds Castle is 7 miles east of Maidstone off Junction 8 of the M20. Coaches run direct from London Victoria coach station and trains run from London Victoria train station to Bearsted from where a connecting coach service operates.

**Concessions**
Children 5–15 years; under 5s free
Families
Over 60s
Students

**Facilities**

**INTERESTING FACT**
Henry VIII visited Leeds Castle with his wife Catherine of Aragon and their entire court, while travelling to the Field of Cloth of Gold tournament in 1520.

*above Leeds Castle, viewed across the lake.*

courtiers and the palace passed out of royal hands. The castle's last owner, Olive, Lady Baillie, was the daughter of a wealthy American socialite; she refurbished the castle and bequeathed it to the nation.

Leeds Castle has Norman foundations, a medieval gatehouse, a Tudor tower and a nineteenth-century country house. Entry is gained via a stone bridge, which originally would have been a wooden drawbridge. The gatehouse accommodated servants and horses as well as providing fortification against attack. The castle is filled with stunning art and antiques gathered by Lady Baillie on her frequent trips to Europe. Her dressing room from the 1930s is perfectly preserved.

Black swans – the symbol of the castle – were imported from Australia by Lady Baillie, who loved birds. Many rare and endangered species can be seen today along with all sorts of wild birds in the Duckery. In the grounds visitors can enjoy the Culpeper Garden, a large cottage garden named after the family who owned the castle in the seventeenth century. There is also a yew maze and an underground grotto.

# Rochester Castle

**Rochester Castle is one of the best preserved examples of Norman architecture in England. It was built on the highest part of the Roman city wall to defend the crossing of the river Medway.**

The first castle on the site was built at the time of the Norman Conquest and is mentioned in the Domesday Book. The fortification was rebuilt in stone between 1087 and 1090 by Gundulf, Bishop of Rochester, for King William Rufus at a cost of £60.

The enormous Norman keep tower, which still stands today, was built *c.*1127 by William of Corbeil, Archbishop of Canterbury after Henry I gave him custody of the castle. This was not just a fortress; it was a palatial residence for the most powerful churchman in the country. Ornately decorated fireplaces and arches bear testament to his status and can still be seen today.

This custodial arrangement led to trouble in 1215 during the dispute between King John and his barons. The archbishop argued with the king and fled the country, leaving the castle to fall into the hands of the king's enemies, which led to an epic siege. King John undermined the outer wall then dug a tunnel under the keep's south-eastern tower. He started a fire using the fat of forty pigs to burn the timber pit props in the tunnel, which brought its southern corner down. Incredibly the castle held out for a further two months until its defenders were starved into submission. The tower was rebuilt in a more robust style inspired by the architecture seen by the Crusaders.

Rochester Castle was rebuilt under Henry III and Edward I and was used as a fort in the fifteenth century, but by the sixteenth century it had fallen into disrepair.

It passed into private hands in the seventeenth century, but continued to deteriorate. The Corporation of Rochester purchased the site in 1884 and turned it into a public pleasure garden.

*opposite Rochester Castle.*

**Rochester Castle**
**Rochester**
**Kent**
**ME1 1SW**

**Tel 01634 402276**
**www.medway.gov.uk/tourism**

**Opening**
Open daily except 24–26 December and New Years Day. Disabled access is limited; please check the website.

**Getting There**
The castle is located in the heart of Rochester, which is just off junction 1 of the M2. Trains run from London Victoria to Rochester station – the castle is a 15-minute walk from the station. Many local buses run past it.

**Concessions**
Children 5–15 years; under 5s free
Families
Over 60s, Students

**Facilities**

**INTERESTING FACT**
Rochester Castle is the tallest Norman keep in the country; it stands 34.5 metres high and has walls that are 3.5 metres thick.

# Stirling Castle

Stirling Castle is an imposing building, dominating the skyline for many miles around. It towers over some of Scotland's most significant battlefields, including Stirling Bridge, the site of William Wallace's victory over the English in 1297 and Bannockburn, where the English were again defeated, this time by Robert the Bruce.

Stirling has provided the backdrop for many colourful events throughout Scottish history and has witnessed assassinations, kidnappings, imprisonments and plenty of political intrigue. Its strategic position highlights the reason for its bloody past, guarding as it does the lowest crossing point of the river Forth, essential for anyone wanting to control central Scotland. The castle has been besieged or attacked sixteen times and three battles have been fought in its immediate vicinity, two of which were turning points in Scottish history.

The Stewart kings – James IV, V and VI – all left behind a great architectural legacy. James IV built the King's House, the Great Hall and the Chapel Royal and ordered the building of the magnificent defensive forework. James V built the palace, work on which was completed by his widow Mary of Guise (who was also Mary Queen of Scots' mother). She also ordered the construction of a line of defences across the neck of the forework, notably the French Spur, which projected from the eastern end of the defences and made it possible to fire from the east and south as well as the main line of the castle.

Mary Queen of Scots was crowned in the Chapel Royal in 1543 and James VI of Scotland (James I of England) was baptised there. However James VI oversaw the rebuilding of the Chapel Royal, which was used for the baptism of his first son, Prince Henry.

**Stirling Castle**
**Stirling**
**FK8 1EJ**

**Tel 01786 450000**
**www.historic-scotland.gov.uk**

**Opening**
Daily except for Christmas Day and Boxing Day.

**Getting There**
Stirling Castle sits at the head of Stirling's historic old town just off the M9. Trains run to Stirling and the castle is a 10-minute walk from the station.

**Concessions**
Children 5–15 years; under 5s free
Over 60s
Unemployed

**Facilities**

The castle has played a significant role in Scotland's history and offers an insight into the life and times of its troubled monarchy.

*opposite* Stirling Castle from the Kings Knott.

**INTERESTING FACT**
In September 1507 John Damian, James IV's alchemist, fell from the castle walls while attempting a flight to France with wings made of hen's feathers.

# Tattershall Castle

This stunning fortified and moated red-brick tower was built for the Lord Treasurer of England, one Ralph Cromwell, between 1433 and 1443. The tower is a landmark of the Fens and it can be seen for many miles around. It is not known how many bricks were used in total to construct the tower, but half a million were specially made at Edlington Moor Brickworks in 1434–35. The cost of these bricks, including transportation was £115.

The castle was last used as a residence in 1700 and was left to decay. It was purchased by an American in 1911, who planned to dismantle the castle piece by piece, ship it to the United States and rebuild it. Visitors could go to the castle and see the destruction taking place as the beautiful Ancaster limestone fireplaces were removed; these were so fine that they had been copied for the Houses of Parliament. The plans for removal provoked an outcry, and letters were sent to *The Times*. Lord Curzon intervened and was offered a deal; if he could arrange a purchase within twenty-four hours the castle would be his. He succeeded and after six months of further negotiations rescued the fireplaces from London and restored them to Tattershall amidst great rejoicing. These can now be seen in the four great chambers, which also contain brick vaulting and great tapestries. The stone shield from over the door was recovered from the cowshed of a nearby farmhouse. Tattershall Castle was bequeathed to the nation in 1925.

There are spectacular views across the Fens from the battlements, with Lincoln Cathedral and the Boston Stump visible on clear days. The guardhouse contains a museum created by Lord Curzon to display finds he gathered while digging out the moat.

*opposite Tattershall Castle.*

**Tattershall Castle**
**Tattershall**
**Lincoln**
**Lincolnshire**
**LN4 4LR**

**Tel 01526 342543**
**www.nationaltrust.org.uk**

**Opening**
Open daily except for Thursdays and Fridays from March – October. Open weekends only through November and December. Disabled access is limited; please check the website.

**Getting There**
Tattershall Castle is 10 miles south-west of Horncastle and is just off the A153. Lincoln and Boston are the main stations; Ruskington, the closest local railway station, is ten miles from the castle. Buses from Ruskington are infrequent.

**Concessions**
Children 5–15 years; under 5s free
Families

**Facilities**

**INTERESTING FACT**
The castle was used as a look-out during the Napoleonic Wars. A soldier was on duty with a tar barrel on one of the turrets, to be lit in the event of invasion.

# Eilean Donan Castle

Eilean Donan Castle sits on a rocky promontory at the meeting of three sea lochs; Loch Long, Loch Duich and Loch Alsh. It is a fortress of solid stone in a wonderfully romantic location. It fought off Norse and Danish coastal raiders and later witnessed scenes of ferocious clan warfare.

At the beginning of the seventh century St Donan lived on the island as a religious hermit; the name Eilean Donan means simply Island of Donan.

The fortified stronghold at Eilean Donan was established during the reign of Alexander II (1214–1250) and it was one of the most important strongholds along the western seas.

The earls of Ross built the castle, but lost it to a family member, one Kenneth McKenzie, the Baron of Kintail. In the early fourteenth century Robert the Bruce was given refuge in the castle; in 1331 when his fortunes had improved he sent his son Randolph, Earl of Moray and Warden of Scotland to Kintail.

The castle was a focus of unrest and retribution until a Jacobite plot in 1719 resulted in its destruction.

**Eilean Donan Castle**
**Dornie by Kyle**
**Ross Shire**
**IB40 8DX**

**Tel 01599 555202**
**www.eileandonancastle.co.uk**

**Opening**
Daily from mid-March to mid-November.
Please check website for further information.

**Getting There**
Eilean Donan Castle is located 8 miles from the Kyle of Lochalsh on the A87 road near the Isle of Skye. Buses run from Glasgow and Inverness.

**Concessions**
Children 6–18 years; under 6s free
Families
Over 60s
Students, Unemployed

**Facilities**

### SPECIAL FEATURE
A miniature of Bonnie Prince Charlie and a lock of his hair are exhibited, as well as a letter he wrote to the clan chiefs in August 1745.

It remained a picturesque ruin until it acquired a new owner, Lt Colonel MacRae-Gilstrap who restored the castle between 1912 and 1932. It now contains an amazing collection of furniture, art and objects, such as John MacRae's sword used in the American War of Independence and at Culloden.

*left The approach to Eilean Donan castle.*

# Palaces

# Chatsworth

Chatsworth is the most impressive palace with a staggering 297 rooms that sit under a roof stretching across an area of 1$\frac{1}{3}$ acres. The park spreads over 100 acres while the entire estate covers 35,000 acres.

The original house was the work of Bess of Hardwick (see Hardwick Hall, pages 160-161) in the sixteenth century. The first Duke rebuilt Chatsworth in classical style between 1686 and 1707 using the leading artists and craftsmen of the day. The house contains one of Europe's finest art collections as well as exquisite furniture, silver, porcelain and sculpture displayed in the grandeur of the first duke's Painted Hall, the State Apartments, the nineteenth-century library, the Great Dining Room and the Sculpture Gallery. The State

**Chatsworth**
**Bakewell**
**Derbyshire**
**DE45 1PP**

Tel 00246 565300
www.chatsworth.org

**Opening**
Open daily from mid-March to mid-December; please check the web site for details.

**Getting There**
Chatsworth is just 4 miles from Bakewell. The nearest train stations are Matlock and Chesterfield and local buses run from the stations regularly.

**Concessions**
Children 5–16 years; under 5s free
Families
Over 60s, Students

**Facilities**

Apartments have recently been restored and, together with the magnificent royal State Bed, returned to their original glory.

The garden is a magical landscape, beautiful in all seasons and can be visited separately from the house. Queen Mary's bower takes its name from Mary Queen of Scots, who was held captive in the house and often spent time in the little garden at the top of the thirty steps. The park was landscaped by the fourth duke between 1790 and 1858 and Capability Brown was engaged to reshape the formal garden. The sixth duke employed Joseph Paxton to work on the gardens and

create the Emperor Fountain, which is capable of throwing a jet of water 150 feet in the air. He also designed the Lily House, on which he based his design for Crystal Palace.

Chatsworth is famous for its waterworks, which include the twenty-four steps of the 300-year-old Cascade, falling 200 yards down the hill, the magic of water shooting from the branches of the willow-tree fountain, the trough waterfall, and Revelation, the water-powered sculpture. There are a huge maze, rose gardens, cottage gardens and kitchen gardens, as well as a new sensory garden.

### SPECIAL FEATURES
Famous curiosities include royal thrones, a giant ancient Greek marble foot, the fan of a Rolls Royce jet engine, and a *trompe l'oeil* painting of a violin hanging on a door.

*above* The bridge and house at Chatsworth.
*overleaf* Chatsworth house.

# Hampton Court

Between 1515 and 1521, Cardinal Wolsey transformed a medieval manor on the site of what is now Hampton Court Palace. It is not known exactly what the original construction looked like, but the evidence suggests that it was designed along the lines of Italian Renaissance palaces, around symmetrical courts and formal gardens and with grand apartments on the first floor.

It was said at the time that Wolsey's palace outshone those of his king, Henry VIII. When Wolsey fell from favour in the early 1520s, Henry took Hampton Court for himself and started an extensive programme of re-modelling. The Great Hall is said to be the last medieval hall built for an English monarch. He also installed a tennis court, which is still in use.

Succeeding rulers tweaked the palace, but the next significant change was made by William and Mary

who added a new wing, partly under the supervision of Christopher Wren. Then George II and Queen Caroline commissioned architects such as William Kent for extensive renovations.

Hampton Court has set the scene for many historic occasions. It was here that James I reached the agreement with the Puritans that led to the King James Bible. Henry VIII's third wife, Jane Seymour, died here and his fourth, Catherine Howard, was

**Hampton Court Palace
Surrey
KT8 9AU**

**Tel 0870 752 7777 (recorded info)
Tel 0870 751 5175 (Historic Royal Palaces
switchboard)
www.hrp.org.uk/HamptonCourtPalace**

**Opening**
The palace and gardens are open daily throughout the year, with the exception of December 24 – 26 and New Year's Day. The park is open all year.

**Getting There**
There is a train station at Hampton Court. Trains run from London Waterloo. Buses run from Richmond BR and Underground station, and numerous local areas in Surrey and central London.

**Concessions**
Children under 16 years
Families
Over 60s
Students

**Facilities**

**SPECIAL FEATURE**
The Maze was originally hornbeam, though it has been repaired in many different plant varieties. It covers a third of an acre and half a mile of paths.

arrested here for adultery. Both ghosts haunt the palace, along with many others – most recently one apparently caught on CCTV, slamming some firedoors.

*opposite* The grand facade of Hampton Court Palace.

# Linlithgow Palace

The imposing ruins of Linlithgow Palace are set on a small hill in a park beside a loch. It was home to numerous kings and queens of Scotland, a resting place to Oliver Cromwell and the birthplace of Mary Queen of Scots.

Edward I of England took possession of a manor house at Linlithgow in 1301, fortifying it with earth and wood. On his defeat at Bannockburn it was reclaimed by the Scots; legend has it that one William Bunnock smuggled eight men into the castle concealed in a hay cart, and that together they took the castle.

Linlithgow Palace
Kirk Gate
Linlithgow
West Lothian
EH49 7AL

Tel 01506 842896
www.historic-scotland.gov.uk

**Opening**
Open daily, except 25–26 December and 1–2 January. Disabled access is limited, please check the website for further information.

**Getting There**
Linlithgow Palace is between Edinburgh and Stirling, just off junction 3 of the M9. There is a regular train service from both Edinburgh and Glasgow mainline stations and the castle is a 5-minute walk from the local train station.

**Concessions**
Children 5–15 years; under 5s free
Over 60s
Unemployed

**Facilities**

David II and Robert III of Scotland continued the building process, but the castle and most of the town were destroyed by fire in 1424. This triggered a building programme that continued for the next 200 years until the square layout seen today was achieved. The west range was the last section to be completed and contained the royal apartments for James IV and his queen, Margaret Tudor, Henry VIII's sister.

James V tinkered with the entrance, moving it to the south range. His queen, Marie de Guise Lorraine, compared Linlithgow Palace favourably to the most splendid palaces found in France. Their daughter Mary (Mary Queen of Scots), was born at Linlithgow in 1542; her father died just six days after her birth.

Henry VIII's plan to marry his son Edward to Mary, in order to unite England and Scotland, was opposed. Undeterred Henry invaded Scotland (an unchivalrous action known as the 'rough wooing'), defeating the Scots at the Battle of Pinkie in 1547. The French helped the Scots, on condition that Mary was sent to France for safe-keeping. She sailed from Scotland aged six, returning a widow thirteen years later.

The last royal visitor was Bonnie Prince Charlie in 1745. After his defeat George II's son, the Duke of Cumberland, took Linlithgow Palace for the English. When they departed in February 1746 a fire was left unattended and within hours the palace was the roofless shell we see today.

**INTERESTING FACT**
In 1513 James IV marched on northern England, leaving his wife Margaret Tudor keeping vigil high on the north-west tower. She waited in vain, for he died at Flodden.

*above* Linlithgow Palace in West Lothian.

# Blenheim Palace

Blenheim Palace, home to the 11th Duke of Marlborough and birthplace of Winston Churchill, is a masterpiece of baroque architecture and has been nominated a World Heritage Site. The house was built to commemorate John Churchill's victory over the French during the Wars of the Spanish Succession. Queen Anne and a grateful nation granted Marlborough the Manor of Woodstock and promised funds to build a house, although these soon dried up and the duke had to complete the building at his own expense.

The palace was designed by John Vanbrugh and building began in 1705. Vanbrugh, who was not a trained architect, was ably assisted by the more practical Nicholas Hawksmoor. The building was far from trouble free, as the first duchess wanted a country house designed for comfort and not for status; eventually Vanbrugh resigned. From the grandeur and detail of the State Rooms to the imposing size of the Great Hall, the palace is steeped in history.

Look for the magnificent Blenheim Tapestry showing Marlborough in his hour of triumph, the painted ceilings by Louis Laguerre in the Saloon and the stucco decoration and false domes in the Long Library. There are collections of Meissen and Sevres porcelain, Boulle furniture, beautiful stone work by Grinling Gibbons and an impressive array of paintings and sculpture.

The fourth duke brought in 'Capability' Brown and William Chambers to fulfil his vision for the park and gardens, and in the 1920s the ninth duke of Marlborough employed the French landscape architect Achille Duchêne to redesign the formal gardens to produce the majestic design we see today.

**INTERESTING FACT**
Winston Churchill proposed to Miss Clementine Hozier at Blenheim in summer 1908 at The Temple of Diana overlooking the lake; she became his devoted wife.

**Blenheim Palace**
**Woodstock**
**Oxfordshire**
**OX20 1PX**

Tel 01993 811091
www.blenheimpalace.com

**Opening**
Daily from February – October, Wednesday – Sunday only from October – December.

**Getting There**
Blenheim Palace is situated in Woodstock, 8 miles from Oxford.

**Concessions**
Children 5–15 years; under 5s free
Families
Over 60s

**Facilities**

The fabulous water terraces are reminiscent of the Parterre d'Eau at Versailles. There are impressive fountains and sculptures, a Rose Garden, an Italian Garden and a Secret Garden, created to celebrate the tercentenary in 2004 of the Battle of Blenheim, and the Grand Cascade.

*opposite and overleaf Views of Blenheim Palace.*

# Kensington Palace

Kensington Palace is a working royal residence, a favourite amongst sovereigns until 1760 and Queen Victoria's birthplace and childhood home. More recently it was the setting for the public to lay floral tributes upon the death of Diana, Princess of Wales.

In 1689 William III bought a Jacobean mansion, originally known as Nottingham House from the Earl of Nottingham. He commissioned Sir Christopher Wren to extend and improve the house. This involved the construction of Royal Apartments, a Council Chamber, the Chapel Royal and the Great Stairs.

The King's staircase features a series of paintings by William Kent depicting a lively eighteenth-century court full of intriguing characters such as Peter the Wild Boy. Kent also decorated other rooms in the king's apartments.

Queen Victoria received news of her accession in her bedroom here, a servant standing by with smelling salts. She held her first Privy Council in the Palace's Red Saloon. Queen Mary, grandmother of the present queen was born at Kensington Palace in 1867 and the Duke of Edinburgh stayed here in his grandmother's apartment in 1947 between his engagement and his marriage.

Today, Kensington Palace State Apartments give visitors insight into the rooms once used by resident monarchs. They are also home to the Royal Ceremonial Dress Collection, with items of royal, ceremonial and court dress on display dating from the eighteenth century to the present day, including a selection of Princess Diana's famous dresses. A series of rooms in Apartment 1A, most recently home to Princess Margaret, can be enjoyed on pre-booked tours. The rooms where the Princess entertained her guests are on show, as well as the kitchen with its fantastic cooker hood specially designed by Lord Snowdon. A walk through the lavish baroque State Apartments of King William III and Queen Mary II offers a different view of royal life.

*opposite* Kensington Place and Gardens.

**Kensington Palace State Apartments**
**Kensington Gardens**
**London W8 4PX**

Tel 0870 751 5170
www.hrp.org.uk

**Opening**
Open daily except 24–26 December.

**Getting There**
Nearest Underground stations are Queensway and High Street Kensington. Buses 70, 94, 148 and 390 run to Bayswater Road and buses 9, 10, 49, 52, 70 and 148 run to Kensington High Street.

**Concessions**
Children 5–16 years; under 5s free
Families
Over 60s, Students

**Facilities**

# The Palace of Holyroodhouse

The Palace of Holyroodhouse is the Queen's official residence in Scotland. It is closely associated with Scotland's turbulent past, though it was founded as an Augustinian monastery by David I in 1128.

As Edinburgh established itself as Scotland's capital city, her monarchs chose to live at Holyroodhouse instead of the rather dark and gloomy Edinburgh Castle. In 1501 James IV cleared the ground close to the abbey and built a palace for himself and his bride, Margaret Tudor; only the gatehouse survives from this period. The Royal Apartments reflect the changing tastes of successive monarchs and offer a revealing insight into royal life through the centuries. Mary Queen of Scots, daughter of James V, spent much of her turbulent reign at the palace and married two of her husbands in the abbey.

The palace fell into decline under James VI and was extensively damaged during the Civil War when Oliver Cromwell's troops were billeted there. In 1745 'Bonnie Prince Charlie' took up residence and used Holyroodhouse as his headquarters during the uprising of that year.

No further renovations took place until the early nineteenth century when George IV made a state visit to Scotland in 1922. He ordered that Mary Queen of Scots' apartments be preserved.

After her purchase of Balmoral, Queen Victoria revived the custom of royalty staying at Holyroodhouse. King George V and Queen Mary continued to visit, installing electricity and bathrooms.

The longest and largest room in the palace is The Great Hall which is decorated with 89 of the original 110 Jacob de Wet portraits of both the real and legendary Kings of Scotland from Fergus I to Charles II. The Royal Apartments are famous for their fine plasterwork ceilings and magnificent furnishings, in particular an impressive collection of Brussels tapestries. The Queen's Gallery houses a programme of changing exhibitions of the most delicate works of art from the Royal Collection.

*opposite* The Palace of Holyroodhouse.

# The Royal Pavilion

The Royal Pavilion in Brighton derives its unique character from the man for whom it was built, George IV. Its magnificent interior is a reflection of his personality and the decadency of the Regency period. The Royal Pavilion was conceived as a monument to style, finesse, technological excellence and, above all, pleasure.

George first arrived in the newly fashionable resort of Brighton in 1783 to escape the stuffy formality of the court of his father, George III. He quickly set about transforming his Brighton house. Various architects worked on the project, but it was not until after George was declared regent in 1811 that he was unfettered by financial constraint and able to effect the transformation he desired.

George first employed architect Henry Holland who turned the original farmhouse into a neoclassical villa,

but he subsequently turned to John Nash to realise his dream. Nash superimposed a cast–iron frame onto the existing building to create a vista of minarets, domes and pagodas. George later used Nash to transform Buckingham House into Buckingham Palace.

The interior was designed to impress and is unashamedly ostentatious and theatrical in spirit. Frederick Crace and Robert Jones employed every decorative conceit and ornamental illusion on the interior – iron cast as bamboo, painted glass ceilings, and strategically placed mirrors to alter perspective.

The ostentation provides a sumptuous sensory experience; look for the domed ceiling of gilded scallop–shaped shells in The Music Room and revel in the loud pink and blue colours in the Long Gallery. No expense was spared on the interior, from the palm-leaf capitals that top the cast-iron columns of the Great Kitchen to the nine lotus-shaped chandeliers in the Music Room. After George IV's death both William IV and Queen Victoria visited the palace before it was sold in 1850 to the local council, who today oversee a rolling programme of restoration and renovation.

*opposite* Brighton's lavish Royal Pavilion.

**The Royal Pavilion
Brighton
BN1 1EE**

Tel **01273 290900**
**www.royalpavilion.org.uk**

**Opening**
Daily except Christmas Eve, Christmas Day and Boxing Day.

**Getting There**
The Pavilion is just off Grand Parade in Brighton and within walking distance of the train station. Trains and coaches run to Brighton from London.

**Concessions**
Children 5–15 years; under 5s free
Families, Over 60s

**Facilities**

# Scone Palace

Scone Palace has a long and distinguished history dating back 1500 years to when it was the capital of the Pictish kingdom and the hub of the Celtic church. It has been immortalized in *Macbeth*, has housed parliaments and witnessed the coronations of numerous kings.

The 100-acre grounds alone are of great significance. In the ninth century Kenneth McAlpin created the kingdom of Scone uniting the Picts and the Scottish Celts to create Scotland as we know it. All Scottish kings were crowned at Scone (pronounced Scoon) thereafter, seated on the celebrated Stone of Scone on Moot Hill, (also known as the Stone of Destiny). The stone was removed by Edward I in 1296 and taken to Westminster – a replica now marks the original site. Scone was the seat of Scottish parliaments and an important power base between 1210 and 1452.

**Scone Palace**
**Perth**
**Tayside**
**PH2 6BD**

**Tel 01738 552300**
**www.scone-palace.co.uk**

**Opening**
1 April – 31 October yearly.

**Getting There**
2 miles north of Perth on the A93; trains and coaches run to Perth then local buses.

**Concessions**
Children 5–15 years; under 5s free
Families
Over 60s

**Facilities**

Scone was destroyed by a mob in 1559; the current gothic palace was built on the remains. The oldest part, the Long Gallery, dates back to 1580 and can boast many royal visitors: Charles II, the Old Pretender, Prince James Edward Stewart, his son Bonnie Prince Charlie and Queen Victoria, who witnessed a demonstration of curling on the Gallery's highly polished floor.

The state rooms are impressive with their portraits by Reynolds and Van Eyck, porcelain from Sevres and Meissen and furniture by Chippendale and Robert Adam. All sorts of curios can be seen; a beautiful writing desk given to the second Earl of Scone by Marie Antoinette; a bed hanging worked on by Mary Queen of Scots during her imprisonment at Loch Leven Castle, and an oak armchair used by Charles II for his coronation. The newest addition to the Palace Gardens is the Murray Star Maze which uses 2000 beech trees to create a stunning tartan maze.

*opposite View across the parkland to Scone Palace.*

# Buckingham Palace

Buckingham Palace is perhaps the most famous palace in the world today. It serves as the office and London residence of Her Majesty the Queen. The State Rooms are used extensively by the royal family on ceremonial and official occasions.

Buckingham Palace evolved from a small town house owned by the dukes of Buckingham, which George III purchased in 1761 for his wife, Queen Charlotte. On his accession, George IV decided to reconstruct the house and asked his architect John Nash to undertake the transformation. Parliament agreed to pay £150,000, but George pressed for a more realistic figure of £450,000. Nash retained the main block but doubled its size.

The remodelled rooms are the State and semi-State rooms, which remain virtually unchanged since Nash's time. Many of the pieces of furniture and works of art in these rooms were bought or made for Carlton House, George IV's London house before his accession.

Neither George IV nor William IV moved into the palace. Queen Victoria was the first sovereign to take up residence, three weeks after her accession. Her marriage to Albert soon showed the shortcomings of the design: there were no nurseries and too few bedrooms. The solution was to move the Marble Arch to its present location at Hyde Park's north-east corner, and build a fourth wing, thereby creating a quadrangle. The costs were largely covered by the sale of George IV's Royal Pavilion at Brighton (see pages 84-85).

The palace contains 775 rooms, including 19 State rooms, 52 royal and guest bedrooms, 188 staff bedrooms, 92 offices and 78 bathrooms. Only the 19 State Rooms are open to the public; these are lavishly furnished with some of the greatest treasures from the Royal Collection, featuring works of art by Rembrandt, Rubens, Vermeer, Poussin and Canaletto, sculpture by Canova and Chantrey and exquisite Sèvres porcelain.

*opposite Buckingham Palace, from St James's Park.*

**Buckingham Palace
London
SW1A 1AA**

**Tel: 020 7766 7300
www.royalcollection.org.uk**

**Opening**
The nineteen State Rooms are open to visitors during August and September. Annual dates should be checked on the website as these vary slightly each year. It is best to book tickets in advance via the website; wheelchair users are always advised to book in advance.

**Getting There**
Buckingham Palace can be reached from several Underground stations: Charing Cross, Victoria, Green Park and Hyde Park Corner. Buses 11, 211, 239, C1 and C10 stop on Buckingham Palace Road.

**Concessions**
Children 5–17 years; under 5s free
Families, Students
Over 60s

**Facilities**

### INTERESTING FACT
Marble Arch originally stood at the centre of Buckingham Palace's courtyard and was designed to celebrate the British victories at Trafalgar and Waterloo.

# Falkland Palace

Falkland has been a royal palace since Stuart times, when King James II of Scotland took it over in the mid-fifteenth century. Previously it had belonged to the Macduff family. It had been a defensive post in even earlier times, but had evolved into a sporting base. The palace is still associated with the sport of falconry; the surrounding woodlands were also ideal for hunting stag and wild boar. Between 1501 and 1541, James IV and James V replaced the earlier castle, although traces of the original can still be seen in the grounds. In its place they built what is acknowledged to be one of the finest Renaissance palaces in Europe. Now restored, the roofed south range contains the chapel royal; this range and the ruined east range surround the central courtyard. The keeper's apartments and the gatehouse have also been restored. The palace contains impressive portraits of the Stuart monarchs and two sets of seventeenth-century tapestry hangings.

The garden was designed by Percy Cane between 1947 and 1952. It includes a wide lawn and the original tennis court made in 1539 and thought to be the oldest in Britain. There's also a herb garden featuring quotations from John Gerard's *Herbal*, published in 1597.

Falkland was at the centre of Scottish politics for a century and a half. In 1402, the Duke of Rothesay was imprisoned in the palace by his uncle and eventually starved to death. James V was ill at the palace when he heard of his daughter's birth; he later died there in 1542. His daughter, Mary Queen of Scots, saw the palace as a refuge from the pressures of court politics in Edinburgh. But Falkland's era of greatness came to an end in 1603 at the union of the crowns, when James VI took his court to London. Charles I and II both visited Falkland, but it gradually fell to decay. In 1887, the Keeper, John Patrick Crichton Stuart, began restoration.

*opposite The gardens at Falkland Palace.*

---

**Falkland Palace
Cupar
Fife, KY15 7BU**

Tel 0844 4932186
www.nts.org.uk

**Opening**
The palace and gardens are open daily from March to October. Check website for further details.

**Getting There**
The palace is in the village of Falkland, 11 miles north of Kirkcaldy. The nearest railway station is at Markinch, near Glenrothes. Local buses run from there.

**Concessions**
Children
Families
Groups (pre-booked)

**Facilities**

---

**SPECIAL FEATURE**
The painted ceiling and oak entrance screen in the Chapel Royal are of national artistic and historic importance.

# Gardens

# Kew Gardens

It is impossible to see all of Kew in a one-day visit; the Botanic Garden's 300 acres are rich in heritage and full of iconic buildings. Kew is packed with the most amazing plants gathered from all over the world and it has been declared a World Heritage Site by UNESCO.

Kew started life as the Royal Gardens of Kew Palace, established by Princess Augusta, wife of Prince Frederick, (son and heir of George II who died before his father in 1751). When George III inherited the estate he called upon 'Capability' Brown for the landscaping and employed Joseph Banks, who had accompanied Captain Cook on some of his voyages, as director. Banks despatched botanical collectors around the world to gather rare and interesting specimens, and Kew became a depository for plant species and a centre of botanical research.

After George's death the gardens languished until they were given over to the state in 1840 and the Botanic Gardens were founded in 1841. The Palm House, built by Richard Turner between 1844 and 1848 is regarded as the most important glass and metal structure surviving today, while his Water Lily House, built in 1852 – then the world's widest single span glasshouse – today houses the stupendous Amazonian water lilies. Chamber's Pagoda (1762) and his Orangery (1761) were both built for George's mother Augusta and can still be enjoyed. Kew Palace is the oldest surviving building in the gardens; it was built in 1631 and was the family home of King George III and Queen Charlotte and recently underwent major renovation.

The gardens are a glorious mix of formal gardens, landscaped lawns, water features, an arboretum and stunning greenhouses packed with exotic flora. New additions include the innovative Davies Alpine House and the grass garden, which has over 600 varieties of grasses. Kew still functions as a botanical research centre and maintains the largest plant collection in the world.

*opposite The Pagoda at Kew Gardens.*
*overleaf The Palm House.*

**Royal Botanic Gardens**
**Kew**
**Richmond**
**Surrey**
**TW9 3AB**

**Tel 020 8332 5655**
**www.kew.org**

**Opening**
Open all year except for Christmas Eve and Christmas Day.

**Getting There**
Kew is on the south bank of the river Thames near Richmond. Trains run from London Waterloo to Kew Bridge; the Underground runs to Kew Gardens; buses 65 and 391 run past Kew Gardens.

**Concessions**
Children under 17
Families, Over 60s
Students, Unemployed

**Facilities**

## SPECIAL FEATURE
The Pagoda is a ten-storey-high structure reaching nearly fifty metres; it was the tallest imitation of a Chinese building in Europe and a skyscraper of its day.

# Levens Hall Gardens

The first Levens Hall was built as a defence against Scottish raiders by the de Redman family in 1350; nothing was more elaborate than the pele tower, which still stands, as do some living quarters around the base. The Bellingham family built an Elizabethan house around this original structure. In the 1690s, Colonel James Grahme added two wings to the rear of the house, creating a courtyard, and filled the house with outstanding Jacobean furniture. The last phase of the creation of Levens Hall came with the addition of the Howard Tower in 1820. The house contains historic furniture, paintings by artists such as Van Dyck and Brueghel the Elder, and, in the dining-room, notable embossed Cordoba leather wallcovers. The earliest known example of English patchwork is also on display.

Levens Hall Gardens are an extraordinary feat of topiary, design and planting. The gardens' striking layout is not entirely surprising, since their designer was trained at Versailles. Colonel James Grahme was Privy Purse to King James II. When the king abdicated in 1688, Grahme left court and returned to Levens Hall. He brought with him Guillaume Beaumont, who had not only learnt his trade at Versailles under the great André le Notre, but had already designed the gardens at Hampton Court. Beaumont was responsible for the inventive layout and topiary, with its pyramids, abstract shapes and tall columns reminiscent of giant chessmen; he also installed what is thought to be the first ha-ha in a British garden.

Besides the arresting topiary, the garden boasts a nuttery and herb, rose and fountain gardens. The latter with its pleached limes, was added in 1994 to celebrate the three hundredth annoversary of the gardens at Levens Hall.

Remarkably, although the topiary was re-cut in 1815, the gardens have remained largely unchanged since they were conceived at the end of the seventeenth century.

## SPECIAL FEATURE

The park contains an avenue of oaks, created by Beaumont to reflect the growing interest in park landscaping at the end of the seventeenth century.

Levens Hall
Kendal
Cumbria
LA8 0PD

Tel 01539 560321
www.levenshall.co.uk

**Opening**
The hall and gardens are open April – October, Sunday – Thursday. Further opening times are available from the website.

**Getting There**
Levens Hall is 5 miles south of Kendal, on the A6. It is signposted. There is a station at Oxenholme, about 5 miles away. Trains run direct from Manchester Airport and London Euston. Buses run from Grasmere, Ambleside, Windermere and Lancaster.

**Concessions**
Children
Families
Groups

**Facilities**

*opposite* Levens Hall, from the Topiary Garden.

# Sissinghurst Castle Garden

The unique garden at Sissinghurst Castle in Kent is the creation of the writer Vita Sackville-West and her husband, the diplomat and literary critic Harold Nicholson. They bought the property in 1930, afraid that they were losing control over developments at the nearby Sackville family seat of Knole.

The manor at Sissinghurst dates back to much earlier times. The name is Saxon and means 'clearing in the woods', which gives an idea of the wildness of the surrounding area in early days. A medieval construction was replaced in the mid-sixteenth century by a brick mansion the tower of which, with its octagonal turrets is still the focal point of the garden. Its owner, Sir Richard Baker, created a house sufficiently impressive to merit a visit by Elizabeth I, during one of her royal progresses through the area in 1573. Remnants of this earlier work have been integrated into the garden, including a cottage that was once part of the Tudor manor and several walls. Two arms of the Elizabethan moat remain. The third is now the Moat Lawn. The tower contains the study where Vita Sackville-West wrote and from its roof there is a view down to her rose garden.

The garden design was Harold Nicholson's, but it was his wife who was responsible for the innovative planting schemes. She conceived Sissinghurst garden as a series of intimate outdoor rooms, shaped by red brick walls or hedges of yew, rose or hornbeam. There are hints of the Mediterreanean, particularly in the terracotta pots from Tuscany which line the lime walk, and in the bold planting of figs and vines. A nuttery leads to a herb garden, the contents of which include woad, lovage, rue, apothecary's rose and camphor.

Sissinghurst Castle Garden
Near Cranbrook
Kent
TN17 2AB

Tel 01580 710700
www.nationaltrust.org.uk

**Opening**
The garden is open from March – October, Friday – Tuesday.
Vita Sackville-West's study and the library are open on certain days during that period. See website for further information.

**Getting There**
Sissinghurst is 2 miles north-east of Cranbrook. Trains call at Staplehurst and there is a special bus link to the Garden. Buses also run from Maidstone and Hastings.

**Concessions**
Children 5–16 years
Families

**Facilities**

Sissinghurst's garden was first opened to the public in 1938. Harold and Vita referred to visitors as 'shillingses', since that was the cost of entry. But it was not meant as a derogatory term; Vita wrote of the old-fashioned 'gardeners' courtesy' that existed between herself and her admiring guests.

*opposite Sissinghurst Castle Garden.*

> **SPECIAL FEATURE**
> On one side of the tower is the ghostly White Garden. Here, all the blossoms are white – lavender, clematis and double primrose – and the foliage grey.

# Castle Howard

Castle Howard must rank as one of the most magnificent stately homes and gardens in Britain. Its construction was begun by the third Earl of Carlisle in around 1700, but it was not completed for another 100 years, spanning the lives of three earls and numerous architects and craftsmen.

The famous house is set in 1000 acres of beautiful gardens and the approach, by a five-mile-long avenue, is lined by lime and beech trees and offers glimpses of

**Castle Howard**
**York**
**YO60 7DA**

**Tel 01653 648 333**
**www.castlehoward.co.uk**

**Opening**
Garden open daily except Christmas Day. House open 1st March to 4th November, and for Christmas from 24th November to 16 December. Please check the website for further information.

**Getting There**
Castle Howard is north-east of York just off the A64. Trains and coaches run to York; buses to Castle Howard from April to September.

**Concessions**
Children 4-16 years; under 4s free
Families, Over 60s, Students

**Facilities**

**INTERESTING FACT**
Playwright John Vanbrugh had never designed a building before Castle Howard. He was ably assisted by Christopher Wren's former deputy, Nicholas Hawksmoor.

the pyramid, temple, mausoleum and the house itself in the distance, all combining to offer a delightful mix of architectural inconsistencies. At the head of the drive is the obelisk, which commemorates the victories of the first Duke of Marlborough. To the south west is the walled garden, which contains a rose garden and an ornamental vegetable garden. To the south is the formal south parterre with the Atlas fountain and south lake with the Prince of Wales fountain, while in Ray Wood there are winding paths to enjoy and the Temple of the Four Winds and the Lost Temple of Venus to find.

The house, designed by John Vanbrugh, is asymmetrical in design, partially due to the conflicting views of the Howards who inherited the ongoing project one after the other to produce a stunning baroque/Palladian mix. It is packed with glorious sculptures, tapestries and pictures assembled by successive earls during visits to Europe. Treasures include paintings by Canaletto, Titian, Reynolds and Gainsborough, a screen by William Morris and a fine collection of porcelain and sculpture.

A fire destroyed the dome and damaged nearly twenty rooms in 1940. George Howard, who inherited the house on the death of his two brothers in the Second World War, determined to restore Vanbrugh's architectural masterpiece. The house has been used as the setting for the television adaptation of Evelyn Waugh's novel, *Brideshead Revisited*.

*above* *The Atlas fountain at Castle Howard.*

# Stowe Landscape Gardens

Stowe Landscape Gardens represented a radical move away from previous ideas about garden design. Until the early eighteenth century, gardens had been formal, artificial showcases of man's ability to manipulate nature into strict patterns. Such a garden was constructed at Stowe in the 1690s, influenced heavily by Italian designs popular at the time. None of this original garden now survives.

The landscape garden that we see today evolved over many decades in the eighteenth century, under the influence of some of the most important gardeners and architects of the time, including Lancelot 'Capability' Brown and Sir John Vanbrugh. The house and gardens represent the ambitions of three generations of the Temple-Grenville family, starting with Sir Richard Temple, later Viscount Cobham. His early plans, realised in the 1710s and 1720s under the direction of Charles Bridgeman, have largely disappeared, though the ha-ha — a revolutionary idea at the time and praised by Alexander Pope — remains.

From the 1730s onwards, an increasingly naturalistic approach to garden design replaced the old artificial shapes and planting. There was also a fascination with the ancient past. The result was an idealized natural landscape, with carefully planted woods, valleys and streams, dotted about with artfully designed bridges and temples in ancient styles, and even 'ruins', including The Gothic Temple, whose orange-coloured stone is in stark contrast to the pale classical hues of the other buildings.

The move in this new direction started in earnest in the 1730s, still under the direction of Bridgeman, who was joined by William Kent and James Gibbs. Kent started out as a painter and studied in Italy; both

influences are in evidence at Stowe, the Palladian Bridge being the clearest example. The designers were joined by 'Capability' Brown, who in 1741 became head gardener. With Kent, he changed the remaining formal elements in the estate; the edges of Bridgeman's octagonal pond were softened, the eleven-acre lake was added along with a 'Grecian Valley', and various areas of woodland and abstract landscaping.

The gardens are designed to be seen from different viewpoints as you walk around, with the various buildings and landforms providing satisfying, attractive and sometimes surprising focal points.

*opposite Stowe Landscape Gardens.*

**SPECIAL FEATURE**
The small valley below the house is Brown's representation of The Elysian Fields of Greek mythology, the equivalent of Paradise.

# Tatton Park

Tatton Park is set in one thousand acres of beautiful rolling parkland containing lakes, tree-lined avenues and herds of deer. The gardens are both extensive and varied; the Egerton family who owned the estate extended the garden boundaries farther into the park every time they wanted to indulge their latest horticultural passion. The net result is a collection of gardens within a garden.

The walled garden is currently being restored to its full nineteenth century glory. The fruit and vegetable gardens have been replanted and there are beautiful glasshouses; vineries, pinery (pineapple house), fig and orchid houses. There is a beech maze, first established in 1795 and Charlotte's Garden, named after Lady Charlotte Egerton. This was designed in the gardenesque style to feature non-native plants by the mansion's architect, Lewis Wyatt. There is an Italian terraced garden and a palatial fernery, both designed by Joseph Paxton, originally Head Gardener at Chatsworth and famous for designing Crystal Palace.

At the end of the garden lies Tatton's famous Japanese garden. It was constructed for Alan de Tatton Egerton, Lady Anna's husband between 1910 and 1913. It is in the style of a tea garden and is connected to an island on which stands a Shinto shrine. It has been acknowledged as one of the finest examples of Japanese gardens to be seen in the UK.

In addition to the gardens, Tatton Park's mansion offers a taste of the refined style of the Egerton family over 200 years. The state rooms contain magnificent furniture and paintings while the servant's quarters reveal the harsh domestic realities. The Tudor Hall,

**Tatton Park**
**Knutsford**
**Cheshire**
**WA16 6QN**

**Tel 01625 534400**
**www.tattonpark.org.uk**

**Opening**
Open all year round; High Season (March – October) open daily, Low Season (October – March) Tuesday – Sunday. Closed Christmas Eve and Christmas Day.

**Getting There**
Tatton Park is 2 miles north-east of Knutsford. The nearest train stations are Altrincham and Knutsford; local buses run from Knutsford.

**Concessions**
Children 4–15 years; under 4s free
Families, Over 60s

**Facilities**

built in 1520 by Sir Richard Brereton offers a glimpse of life in an earlier age. Visitors can also sample a taste of farm life at the working farm.

*opposite Tatton Park's Japanese Garden.*

**INTERESTING FACT**
Tatton Park was the inspiration for Cumnor Towers in Elizabeth Gaskell's novel *Wives and Daughters*. Gaskell lived in nearby Knutsford.

# Stourhead

The estate at Stourhead was bought in 1717 by Henry Hoare, of the London banking family. It had previously been the home of the Stourton family for 700 years. Henry Hoare demolished the existing house and built in its place an imposing Palladian creation designed by the architect Colen Campbell.

Stourhead as it is now was largely the creation of Henry's son, Henry Hoare II, who moved there after his mother's death in 1741. For forty years, he worked tirelessly on the gardens, moulding them into the artfully naturalistic sweep of parkland we see today. Like the house, the gardens reflect the eighteenth-century fascination with classical civilization. Their

Stourhead
Stourton
Warminster
Wiltshire
BA12 6QD

Tel 01747 841152
www.nationaltrust.org.uk

**Opening**
The garden is open daily throughout the year. The house and King Alfred's Tower are open from March – October, Friday – Tuesday. For opening times, please see website.

**Getting There**
Stourhead is 3 miles north-west of Mere on the A303. Gillingham railway station is 6 miles away and Bruton 7 miles. On local buses, alight at Zeals, 1.25 miles away.

**Concessions**
Children 5–15 years; under 5s free
Families (2 adults, 3 children)
Pre-booked groups (15 or more)

**Facilities**

centre is a lake, complete with islands, formed by damming the River Stour.

The only professional to work on the gardens with Henry Hoare II was the architect Henry Flitcroft, whose designs provide focal points for the landscape. The Pantheon was made to echo the curves of the lawns around it. Also above the lake is a Temple of Apollo, based on an ancient circular design from Baalbec in Syria. Nestled in the grounds there is the estate village of Stourton, whose cottages stretch down to a Palladian bridge over the lake. On a grander scale there is the famous landmark of Alfred's Tower, a

triangular folly with an internal spiral staircase leading to a viewing platform.

Disturbed by social unrest in London and afraid for the family's assets, in 1780 Henry Hoare II gave Stourhead to his grandson, Richard Colt Hoare, on the condition that he give up all his connections with the bank. Pavilions were added to the house, to provide space for a gallery, a library and extended art collection.

In 1902, a major fire destroyed the central section of the house. The family, staff and neighbours rescued the invaluable art collection.

**SPECIAL FEATURE**
The grotto is a rocky chamber by the lake, linked to anterooms by tunnels. Light is filtered by the water and reflects off the surfaces, making the grotto eerie and restful.

*above The Lake at Stourhead.*

# The Lost Gardens of Heligan

The Lost Gardens of Heligan is a unique estate that lives up to the romance of its name. Heligan was the seat of the Tremayne family for 400 years. By the end of the nineteenth century the gardens were at their zenith with newly imported exotic species flourishing, but it subsequently fell into disuse and became wild and overgrown.

The hurricane of 1990 should have consigned Heligan to being a mere footnote in history, but Tim Smit and John Willis, a Tremayne descendant, explored the derelict gardens. Work started to restore the 200 acres in 1991, funded by grants and public money, and much of the early garden restoration was undertaken by volunteers. The project is now self supporting.

The garden is divided into numerous distinct areas; The Productive Garden encompasses the vegetable garden, the melon yard and the walled flower garden, which between them grow more than 200 varieties of fruit and vegetable and create a wonderful display of edible and ornamental crops.

The Pleasure Gardens conceal a series of romantic structures, a New Zealand garden, an Italian garden, a ravine, a crystal grotto and a sundial garden – all painstakingly restored to their former glory. The gardens house the only working manure-heated pineapple pit in the UK, and are home to vast and beautiful mud sculptures in the woodland.

Heligan is perhaps most famous for its jungle; the steep-sided sub-tropical valley provides a micro-climate for a riot of exotic foliage and stunning trees with four interconnecting ponds which offset the lush foliage. Here you will find the largest collection of tree ferns in Britain and a banana plantation. From the viewing platform at the bottom of the ravine visitors gaze up at an exotic jungle landscape, which transports them to a whole new world.

*opposite Jungle landscape at the Lost Gardens of Heligan.*

**The Lost Gardens of Heligan**
**Pentewan**
**St Austell**
**Cornwall**
**PL26 6EN**

**Tel 01726 845100**
**www.heligan.com**

**Opening**
Open all year round except for Christmas Eve and Christmas Day.

**Getting There**
Situated five miles south of St Austell on the B3273. National trains and coaches run to St Austell, local buses onward to the gardens.

**Concessions**
Children 5–15 years; under 5s free
Families, Over 60s

**Facilities**

**INTERESTING FACT**
The discovery of a motto 'Don't come here to sleep or slumber' dated 1914 and signed by the garden workers, fired an obsession to bring the gardens back to life.

# Knole Gardens

The core of the house and gardens at Knole was built by Thomas Bourchier, Archbishop of Canterbury, in 1456. It was then owned by four more archbishops until the Dissolution of the Monasteries left the property in the hands of Henry VIII. But it was his daughter, Elizabeth I, who passed the house, gardens and park to her cousin, Thomas Sackville, in whose family it has remained to this day.

The house has a network of courtyards with walls of Kentish ragstone. In contrast with the plain, almost rugged, exterior, the interiors are richly decorated and contain furniture and art of some lavishness. The collection was enhanced when the sixth Earl of Dorset, a descendant of Sackville, became Chamberlain to

**Knole House and Park**
**Sevenoaks**
**Kent**
**TN15 0RP**

**Tel 01732 462100**
**www.nationaltrust.org.uk**

**Opening**
House open March – October, Wednesday – Sunday. Garden open on the same dates, Wednesdays only. For further opening dates please telephone or see website.

**Getting There**
Knole is less than a mile from Sevenoaks. Trains from London and the south coast call at Sevenoaks station. Local buses run from Bromley North and Tunbridge Wells, both with train stations.

**Concessions**
Children under 15 years
Pre-booked groups (10 or more)

**Facilities**

William III. King James II's bed, an extraordinary creation in scarlet, silver and gold can currently be seen under restoration.

Archbishop Bourchier installed a small lavender garden at Knole, which was enlarged by Henry VIII, who built the nearly mile-long ragstone walls around it.

From that time to the present day, the garden has been divided into a formal area of lawns and borders, and an informal area known as the wilderness, with paths rambling under beech trees.

*above Deer grazing in Knole Gardens.*

**INTERESTING FACT**
The great storm of 1987 devastated Knole's Park and the gardens. Restoring them to their original state involved the replanting of over 250,000 trees.

# Crathes Castle Garden

Crathes is a sixteenth-century castle with a twentieth-century Arts and Crafts garden. The castle was built over a forty-year period from 1553 by the Burnetts, who had lived in the area since the early fourteenth century. It was in that period that Alexander Burnard (the Burnards later being known as Burnett) was made Royal Forester of Drum by Robert the Bruce, who presented him with the Horn of Leys in 1323. This jewelled heirloom is now on display in the castle and representations of it can be seen on the family coat of arms and throughout the house, including on the laird's bed.

The castle is an L-shaped towerhouse, adorned with turrets and gargoyles. Part of it is a modern two-storey building built to replace an eighteenth-century wing

## SPECIAL FEATURE

The famous June Borders are two beds of herbaceous planting in lavish and dramatic colours, set against the backdrop of the castle.

that burned down in 1966. The rest is the original sixteenth-century structure.

Inside, Jacobean painted oak ceilings have survived, though they were only uncovered in 1877. The most notable is in the Room of the Nine Nobles. The whole of the top floor is taken up by a long gallery, used to display favourite pictures and furniture, and for exercise in bad weather.

There would originally have been a simple kitchen garden at Crathes. It was developed into a walled garden by Sir James and Lady Burnett, 300 years after the castle was completed. The fact that the garden, which is situated on a latitude further north than Moscow, has flourished in an unfriendly climate is testament to the imagination and knowledge behind its creation. The whole actually comprises eight gardens, divided by yew hedges that probably date back to 1702; the avenues of lime trees may be even older. Separate areas within the walls include a flawless croquet lawn, a red garden and a golden garden. The compartmentalised, formal layout, with its linked enclosures and statuary, is a notable example of the Arts and Crafts approach to garden design.

*opposite Winter at Crathes Castle.*

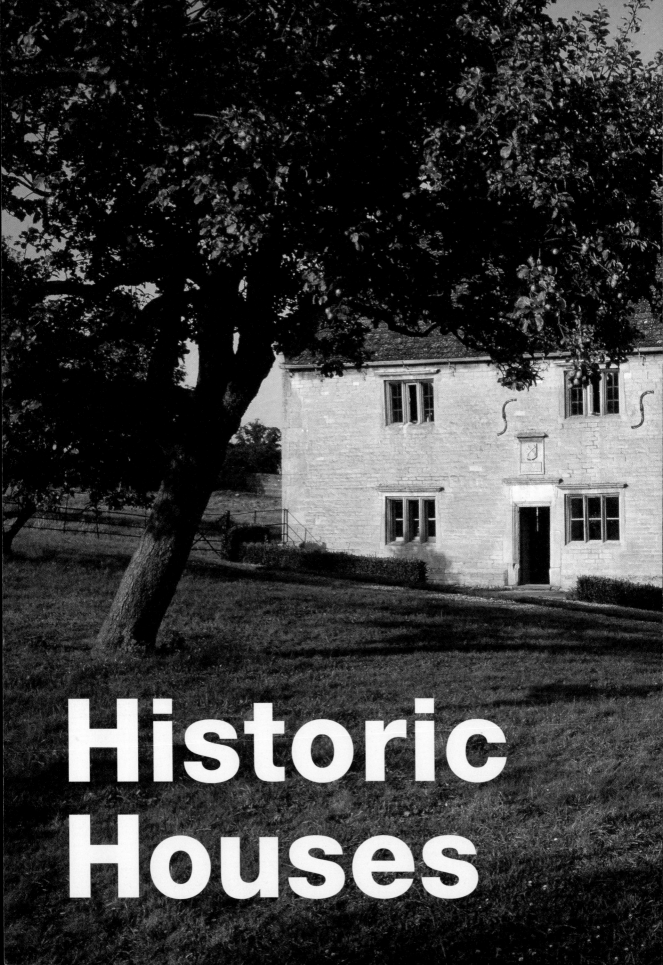

# Historic
# Houses

# Chartwell

The house and gardens at Chartwell are inextricably linked with the life of their most famous owner, Winston Churchill. Yet the house as it stands now is very different in style and atmosphere to the 'modified Elizabethan manor house' he first saw in 1922. It may have been Elizabethan in origin, but the Chartwell of the early 1920s was heavily Victorian in style. With the aid of the architect Philip Tilden, Churchill remodelled the house into a warm, informal family home. Much of the work was done during his political 'wilderness' years in the 1930s when, with no role in government and earning a living from writing history, he had time and energy to devote to the house.

Churchill's major addition was the garden wing, with three large rooms. Outside, he and his wife Clementine created gardens on terraced levels, loosely framed with walls and hedges and planted in simple schemes and gentle colours. Much inspiration was drawn from the Arts and Crafts movement, popular at the time. The rose garden is regarded as a perfect reflection of Clemmie's taste; the high walls were partly built by Churchill himself. The kitchen garden boasts a corridor of roses in thirty-two different shades of gold, planted by the couple's children on the event of their golden anniversary in 1958.

The house contains a number of pictures by Churchill, who used painting as an antidote to the stresses of political life, with a dedicated studio at the bottom of the garden.

One of many mementos of Churchill in the house is the visitors' book, signed by Lloyd George, Balfour and Field Marshal Montgomery, among many others.

*opposite and overleaf* Views of the house at Chartwell.

---

**Chartwell**
**Mapleton Road**
**Westerham**
**Kent**
**TN16 1PS**

**Tel 01732 868381**
**www.nationaltrust.org.uk**

**Opening**
Open Wednesday – Sunday, and bank holidays all year. Closed 24 – 26 December.

**Getting There**
Chartwell is 2 miles south of Westerham. Trains to Edenbridge or Edenbridge Town (4 miles), Oxted or Sevenoaks. Buses from Bromley North, Bromley South, Tunbridge Wells and Oxted.

**Concessions**
Children
Pre-booked groups

**Facilities**

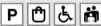

**SPECIAL FEATURE**
Churchill's study is almost exactly as he left it. It was deliberately positioned next to his bedroom, so he could dictate to secretaries at all hours.

# Anne Hathaway's Cottage

**Fans of William Shakespeare will relish the opportunity to enter the world of the poet and playwright to see where he courted and seduced Anne Hathaway, eight years his senior.**

The cottage is the archetypal chocolate-box building with half-timbered walls, latticed windows, thatched roof and dreamy rural location. The 'cottage' is in fact a substantial twelve-roomed farmhouse, properly known as Hewland Farm. The Hathaway family were prosperous and owned ninety acres of land around their house.

The farmhouse was built in the 1460s and extended around 1623. Many original features have been preserved including some fireplaces and the rush bed on which Anne Hathaway was reputedly born. The farmhouse remained in the Hathaway family until 1892 when it was sold to the Shakespeare Birthplace Trust for preservation. The cottage caught fire in 1969 and was severely damaged, but extensive restoration work took place.

Anne never attended school and was, ironically, illiterate. She was 26 when she married, practically an old maid for her day, though scandalously she became pregnant before she was married. Anne's father Richard, who died in 1581, left her £6, 13s 4d to be given to her on the day of her marriage and she married Shakespeare the following year. Anne moved out of the family home and went to live with her in-laws in Stratford. Their daughter Susanna was born in May 1583, six months after the wedding.

Anne Hathaway's Cottage is full of period furniture including the 'second best bed' that Shakespeare famously left to his wife in his will and a fireside settle on which it is believed that he courted Anne. The garden and surrounding countryside are very beautiful and it is possible to follow the footpaths from Stratford to Shottery, which Shakespeare must surely have trodden in order to visit Anne.

*opposite Anne Hathaway's Cottage.*

**Anne Hathaway's Cottage**
**Cottage Lane**
**Shottery**
**Warwickshire**
**CV37 9HH**

**Tel 01789 292100**
**www.shakespeare.org.uk**

**Opening**
Open daily, except 23–26 December. Disabled access is limited; please check the website.

**Getting There**
The cottage is 1 mile outside Stratford-upon-Avon. Trains run from London Marylebone to Stratford-upon-Avon. Local buses and tour buses run regularly to the cottage.

**Concessions**
Children 5–16 years; under 5s free
Families
Over 60s
Students

**Facilities**

> **INTERESTING FACT**
> The graves of Anne and Shakespeare are in Holy Trinity Church, Stratford-upon-Avon. A bust of Shakespeare commissioned by Anne is said to be a good likeness.

# Apsley House

Apsley House was designed by Robert Adam and built between 1771 and 1778 for Baron Apsley, the Lord Chancellor. The house was bought by Richard Wellesley in 1807, but later sold to his younger brother Arthur, the Duke of Wellington. After a celebrated military career, culminating with victory at the Battle of Waterloo in 1815, Apsley House became the London base from which Wellington could pursue his political career.

Adam's original house was made of brick, but the Wellesley family encased it in Bath stone. They also extended it twice, adding the Corinthian portico and two bays to the west wing. Possibly to reflect Wellington's rising status, many rooms were also redesigned in his time, although some Adam interiors remain, including the semicircular staircase and the drawingroom. The house became the perfect setting for impressive entertaining, with the focus on the annual banquets to commemorate Wellington's most famous victory, held in the ninety foot long Waterloo Gallery.

Wellington was a keen art collector. Many of the paintings hanging throughout the first floor came from the Spanish Royal collection, which came into his possession after the Battle of Vitoria in 1813. Besides sixteenth-century Spanish works, there are particularly fine paintings by Dutch and Flemish masters and examples of the nineteenth-century British school. The collection includes four works by Velazquez and important paintings by Goya, Rubens and Brueghel among many others. Wellington was also given numerous unique pieces of silver and porcelain as gifts. His military victories are celebrated in the Wellington Shield and the candelabra presented by the Merchants and Bankers of the City of London. The silver Portuguese service, used at the Waterloo Banquets, has a centrepiece eight metres long. The Sevres Egyptian service was commissioned by Napoleon as a gift for the Empress Josephine.

Apsley House is also known as 'Number One London'; it was the first house reached after the toll gates at Knightsbridge, on the road into London from the west.

*opposite* The lavish interior of Apsley House.

**Apsley House**
149 Piccadilly
London, W1J 7NT

Tel 0207 499 5676
www.english-heritage.org.uk/apsleyhouse

**Opening**
Apsley House is open Tuesdays to Sundays and Bank Holidays. It is closed 24–26 December and New Years Day.

**Getting There**
Hyde Park Corner Underground station is next to Apsley House. Victoria British Rail station is half a mile away. Numerous buses call outside or close to the house.

**Concessions**
Children 5–16 years; under 5s free
Families
Groups (11 or more)
Over 60s
Students, Unemployed

**Facilities**

**SPECIAL FEATURE**
The nude statue of Napoleon holding Nike which stands in the stairwell is by Antonio Canova. Napoleon himself described the statue as 'too athletic'.

# Skara Brae

**Buried on the southern shore of Sandick's Bay, 'O Skaill is the Neolithic village of Skara Brae, one of Britain's most enigmatic ancient sites.**

Built some 5,000 years ago and inhabited for six centuries it offers a tantalizing glimpse of a lost culture that once thrived on the Orkney Islands, north of the Scottish mainland.

The eight single-room houses, inhabited between 3200 BC and 2200 BC, were substantial – more than half the size of a modern two-bed semi – and were linked to each other by passages. The cluster of houses is exceptionally well preserved, with superbly made furnishings and fittings, which would have been crafted using only the most basic tools.

The inhabitants were hunters and farmers who left behind beads and dice that suggest they liked to wear jewellery and to play games much as people do today. But other objects, such as strange carved stones, are a reminder of how little we really know about the villagers' lives.

Viewing platforms allow visitors to look right inside the houses. There is a replica house to explore, plus a virtual tour and a visitor centre.

Near Skara Brae are magnificent Neolithic stone circles and great burial mounds where people may have met for rituals; now we can only guess at their beliefs, gods and practices.

The village was first uncovered by a great storm in 1850, which revealed the outline of a number of stone buildings. The local laird, William Watt of Skaill, began excavations at the site, but it was not until another storm in 1925 that more structures were discovered.

The village is part of the UNESCO Heart of Neolithic Orkney World Heritage Site – a collection of monuments ranked as being as important as the pyramids of Egypt or the Great Wall of China.

*opposite Skara Brae and the Bay of Skaill.*

**Scara Brae Visitor Centre**
**Sandwick**
**Orkney**
**KW16 3LR**

**Tel 01856 841815**
**www.historic-scotland.gov.uk**

**Opening**
Daily except for Christmas Day and New Years Day.

**Getting There**
Skara Brae is 19 miles north-west of Kirkwall, the capital of Orkney, on the B9056. Bicycles can be hired in Stromness.

**Concessions**
Children 5–15 years; under 5s free
Over 60s

**Facilities**

**INTERESTING FACT**
Originally built beside an inland loch, thousands of years of coastal erosion meant Skara Brae survived because it was buried by sand storms.

# Burghley House

Burghley House, one of the greatest Elizabethan mansions, was built between 1555 and 1587 for William Cecil, Lord Burghley, who almost certainly designed it himself. Cecil became Lord Treasurer under Elizabeth I and as one of the most influential and long-serving courtiers in the country he desired a family seat that fitted his status. It is ironic that he was barely able to spend any time at the house.

The house was made in the shape of an 'E' in honour of the queen, although the north-west wing is now missing. The stone came from a local quarry in Northamptonshire. Although the house has been altered over the centuries, the heart of the Tudor building can be seen in the inner courtyard and the gatehouse on the west front, the original grand entrance. In later alterations, the open loggias on the ground floor were enclosed during the seventeenth century and in the eighteenth, under the guidance of Lancelot 'Capability' Brown, the south front was raised to alter the skyline. The north-west wing was demolished to allow a better view of Brown's parkland. In the nineteenth century, a two-storey corridor was added around the inner courtyard, which blocked the view of the courtyard from the state rooms.

There are eighteen state rooms at Burghley House, all containing important works of art and furniture collected over time. The rooms themselves are works of art, the grandest decorated by Antonio Verrio in the seventeenth century. There are several exceptional Italian paintings, four state beds, rare pieces of European porcelain and the earliest inventoried collection of Japanese ceramics in the west. The Pagoda room contains portraits of Elizabeth I and her father, Henry VIII, among others; in the Blue Silk bedroom there is a Virgin and Child by Gentileschi obtained from Pope Clement XIV in exchange for a telescope.

The Heaven Room was decorated by Verrio with scenes of gods and goddesses in a dynamic, three-dimensional effect. Outside, the ceiling over the staircase shows Hell, its entrance the gaping mouth of a huge cat.

*opposite* Burghley House, Lincolnshire.

**Burghley House**
**Stamford**
**Lincolnshire, PE9 3JY**

**Tel 01780 752451**
**www.burghley.co.uk**

**Opening**
Burghley House is open daily, except Friday, from April until the end of October. Further opening details from the website.

**Getting There**
The house is 1 mile from Stamford where there is a train station.

**Concessions**
Children 5–15 years; under 5s free
Families
Groups (pre-booked)
Over 60s
Students

**Facilities**

**SPECIAL FEATURE**
The huge kitchen contains 260 copper utensils and the skulls of turtles used to make soup.

# Lanhydrock

Lanhydrock is a late Victorian house that evolved from very much earlier origins. In 1620, Sir Richard Robartes bought what had once been part of the Priory of St Petroc in Bodmin until the Dissolution of the monasteries, and was then a private estate. Sir Richard and his son John (later Earl Radnor) constructed a traditional square house around a central courtyard, of which only the gatehouse remains.

In the 1780s the east range was demolished to give a 'U' shape, a plan which has been retained. But little else was done to the house for two centuries and it was allowed to fall into decay. Then, in the mid-nineteenth century, the first Baron Robartes of Lanhydrock and Truro, having inherited the estate from his mother, decided to make it his home. He engaged

**SPECIAL FEATURE**
Among the book collection is part of *The Lanhydrock Atlas*, a four-volume survey of the second Earl's Cornish estates at the end of the seventeenth century.

the celebrated architect George Gilbert Scott to remodel the house into a comfortable country home. Only twenty years after the completion of the work, in 1881, all but the north wing was destroyed in a fire. Lady Robartes died a few days later, apparently of shock. Her husband died the following year. Their son Thomas restored the house, with a neo-Jacobean façade in the original material – granite – but with a Victorian interior layout. The architect was Richard Coad, who had been a pupil of Scott's.

Most impressive of the rooms, and a survivor from before the fire, is the long gallery in the north wing. Its plaster ceiling depicting biblical scenes dates from the mid-seventeenth century. The house is furnished in the Victorian style much as it would have been after the last restoration, but also with fine examples of pieces from earlier eras. The servants' areas have also been preserved; the kitchen, larders and dairy still contain the implements the Victorian staff would have used.

Outside, also in Victorian fashion, there are twenty-two acres of formal gardens, with herbaceous borders and parterres decorated with bronze urns brought from Paris in 1857.

*opposite A bronze urn in the garden at Lanhydrock.*

# Cragside

Cragside was the brainchild of the Victorian inventor, William (later Lord) Armstrong. Already a successful Tyneside industrialist, he responded to poor British performance in the Crimean War by developing a new gun. The Armstrong Gun secured his reputation – and his fortune.

Armstrong bought land in the Debdon Valley after visiting the area on holiday. His first house on the site, finished in 1866, was a modest family retreat. But he then engaged the famous architect Richard Norman Shaw. Over the following fifteen years, Shaw transformed Cragside into an impressive mansion – a showcase for some of his most original work.

The rooms Shaw designed first, for use by the Armstrong family, are on an unpretentious scale; the

**Cragside**
**Rothbury**
**Morpeth**
**Northumberland NE65 7PX**

**Tel 01669 620333**
**cragside@nationaltrust.org.uk**

**Opening**
Cragside House is open April – November, Tuesday – Sunday and Bank Holiday Mondays. The gardens are open March – December.

**Getting There**
Cragside is 13 miles south-west of Alnwick and 13 miles north-west of Wooler. There are buses from Morpeth and Newcastle.

**Concessions**
Children 5–16 years; under 5s free
Families (2 adults, up to 3 children)
Pre-booked groups (10 or more)

**Facilities**

library is a welcoming room that boasts beautiful views of the glen. But as one of his generation's most influential industrialists, Armstrong was visited by dignitaries and even royalty. Shaw thus designed his grandest rooms with this in mind. The Owl Suite, with its black walnut bed with owls carved on the posts, alcove with sunken bath and plumbed-in washstand, was occupied at various times by the Shah of Persia, the King of Siam and the Crown Prince of Afghanistan.

But the focus of the house is the drawing room, completed for a royal visit in 1884. Connected to the Owl Suite by an impressive vaulted corridor displaying portraits and statues set against dark red walls, the room is dominated by a monumental carved marble chimney-piece designed by W.R. Lethaby. The rippling veins in the marble around the fireplace echo the harnessed power of water which is such an important feature of Cragside.

Outside, Armstrong blasted the sides of the valley to create dramatic rock formations, around which he planted 688 hectares (1700 acres) of woodland and pleasure gardens. They are home to England's tallest tree, a 59m (193.5ft) Douglas Fir.

*opposite The house at Cragside.*

# Harewood House

Harewood House is a superb eighteenth-century stately home with magnificent Adam interiors. It is home to a wonderful art collection and an impressive collection of Chippendale furniture, fine porcelain and royal memorabilia.

The Harewood House estate was purchased by Edwin Lascelles in 1738. He employed John Carr of York as architect, but his plans for a grand house in the Palladian style were also shown to Robert Adam. Carr designed the central portion of the house while Adam designed the two wings and the interiors. The foundations were laid in 1759 but the house was not habitable for another twelve years. Thomas Chippendale was commissioned to provide all the furniture, although he complained in 1777 that he had worked on Harewood for eight years and been paid almost nothing.

**Harewood House**
**Harewood**
**Leeds**
**West Yorkshire**
**LS17 9LG**

**Tel 0113 218 1000**
**www.harewood.org**

**Opening**
Open daily from March to October. Please check the website for further details.

**Getting There**
Harewood is located at the junction of the A61/A659. The number 36 bus runs to Harewood from Harrogate and Leeds.

**Concessions**
Children 5–16 years; under 5s free
Families, Over 60s

**Facilities**

Changes were made in the nineteenth century by Charles Barry, including the addition of a third storey. The house was remodelled again between 1929 and 1939 by Princess Mary and the sixth Earl with a view to restoration.

The state rooms are impressive; look out for Chippendale's carved wooden pelmets in the gallery. Paintings by El Greco, Titian, Tintoretto, Reynolds, Turner, Girtin and Varley can be seen, as can Sévres porcelain formerly belonging to Louis XV, Louis XVI and Marie Antoinette. Adam drew the ceiling in 1769 and it has been called his finest achievement. Joseph Rose executed the plasterwork and Biaggio Rebecca the paintings.

In 1758 Lancelot 'Capability' Brown designed his trademark undulating landscape for Harewood and in the nineteenth century Charles Barry added a formal terrace and parterre. The bird garden, which sits on 'Capability' Brown's lake, is home to 120 species of exotic, non-native birds, such as the Chilean flamingo. A cascade, which joins the lake to an outgoing stream, is particularly spectacular in spring. The rose garden leads onto the walled garden which is packed with fruit and vegetables, as it has been for over 200 years.

*opposite The impressive frontage of Harewood House.*

# Dove Cottage

**Dove Cottage has passed into literary history as being not just the home of William Wordsworth, but the house in which he wrote his immortal poem 'I Wandered Lonely As A Cloud', also known as 'Daffodils', inspired by a walk round Ullswater.**

Wordsworth first saw Dove Cottage during a walking holiday in the area with his friend Samuel Taylor Coleridge. It is a typical homestead of the area, with walls limewashed to keep out the damp, a slate roof and floors and slate arrangements on the chimneys to stop the smoke blowing back in. In earlier times, it had been a pub – the Dove and Olive – since at least 1617. When William saw it in 1799, it was a house for rent and he and his sister Dorothy moved in in December.

Wordsworth was one of the dominant voices of the Romantic movement, which shifted the emphasis away from intellectual rationalism towards the emotions and imagination. The Romantics focused on nature and man's relationship with the natural world. Dove Cottage was a perfect spot for those preoccupations. It was here that Wordsworth produced much of his formative and best-known work, including 'Intimations of Immortality', 'Ode to Duty' and much of his autobiographical epic, 'The Prelude'. And, of course, 'Daffodils'.

Not surprisingly, the Wordsworths were passionate about the garden and orchard at Dove Cottage. They tended their 'little domestic slip of mountain' with care and skill.

Wordsworth described their days at Dove Cottage as being of 'plain living but high thinking', but the Wordsworths did not live in isolated austerity. Dorothy's meticulous journals note that Coleridge visited, as did Walter Scott, Charles and Mary Lamb, Robert Southey and Thomas de Quincey. In 1802, Wordsworth married a childhood friend, Mary Hutchinson, who also came to live at Dove Cottage. They had three children in four years. Eventually, the house became too small for the growing family and the constant stream of visitors, and they moved to Grasmere.

*opposite Dove Cottage in the Lake District, Wordsworth's home from 1799–1808.*

## SPECIAL FEATURE
The generous larder off the kitchen has a small natural spring under the floor which keeps it cool in summer and frost-free in winter.

# Haddon Hall

Haddon Hall is a fortified medieval manor house dating from the twelfth century and has been owned by the same family since 1567. It is surrounded by beautiful terraced Elizabethan gardens and is situated in the dramatic countryside of the Peak National Park.

Part of the great charm of Haddon is that it avoided many of the architectural and interior-design fashions of the seventeenth and eighteenth century as the family lived elsewhere for 200 years. The house is built of Derbyshire gritstone and limestone and the hall seems originally to have followed the plan of a Norman fort with a curtain wall enclosing a courtyard and a defensive tower. Features such as the banqueting hall and the great chamber were added in the fourteenth century. The long gallery was the project of Sir John

Manners and his wife Dorothy Vernon and is pure Elizabethan in style. The plaster ceiling shows the armorial peacock of the Manners family and the boar of the Vernons.

The earliest recorded royal visitor was Prince Arthur, Henry VIII's eldest brother. Prince Edward (later Edward VII) and Princess Alexandra stayed for lunch, although the house was unoccupied at the time. King George V and Queen Mary visited, as well as Prince Charles and Princess Anne in 1979.

Haddon has a remarkable Tudor kitchen; scorch marks on the timber partition wall show where candles were placed for light on dull winter days and dark evenings.

There are many fine tapestries in the house. The most important are those depicting the five senses, which are believed to have been owned by Charles I, but sold following his execution in 1649.

The beautiful house has provided the backdrop for many costume dramas including both the BBC 2006 adaptation of *Jane Eyre* and the 2006 film of *Pride and Prejudice*.

*opposite The courtyard at Haddon Hall.*

**Haddon Hall**
**Bakewell**
**Derbyshire**
**DE45 1LA**

**Tel 01629 812855**
**www.haddonhall.co.uk**

**Opening**
The house is open daily from May to September and on Saturdays, Sundays and Mondays in April and October. Please check the website for further details.

**Getting There**
Haddon is two miles south of Bakewell on the A6. Matlock is the nearest train station and a local bus service operates from there.

**Concessions**
Children 5–16 years; under 5s free
Families, Over 60s

**Facilities**

# Burns' Cottage

Robert Burns was born in Alloway in 1759 and by the time of his death, at just thirty-seven years of age, he had become Scotland's best loved poet and the symbol of the regeneration of a nation. Burns belongs among a handful of poets, including such luminaries as Shakespeare and Homer, whose work reaches across national, cultural and language barriers.

His father, William, a gardener from Kincardineshire, did his best to ensure that his sons Robert and Gilbert received as good an education as possible. Robert's mother instilled a love of Scottish songs in her son, singing traditional verses to him, and a cousin enthralled him with tales of ghosts and witches. He roamed the Alloway countryside learning about plants, birds and animals.

**Burns' Cottage**
**Burns National Heritage Park**
**Murdoch's Lone**
**Alloway**
**Ayr**
**KA7 4PQ**

**Tel 01292 443700**
**www.burnsheritagepark.com**

**Opening**
Open daily except for Christmas Day, Boxing Day, New Years Day and 2 January.

**Getting There**
35 miles south of Glasgow along M77. Trains to Ayr and local bus service.

**Concessions**
Children 5–15 years; under 5s free
Families
Over 60s, Students

**Facilities**

## INTERESTING FACT
Robert Burns came from modest country stock, in 1757 his father built by hand the two-roomed cottage, or 'but and ben' that Robert was born in, in January 1759.

In 1786 Burns published his first book of poems, the *Kilmarnock Edition*, written in local dialect. He rapidly acquired cult status and became a huge celebrity, fêted wherever he travelled in Scotland.

He later published the *Scots Musical Museum* in which he collected and revised several hundred songs and tunes which may otherwise have been lost for ever. This work helped to generate an interest in Scottish culture across Europe and the world.

He died on 21 July, 1796 and on the fifth anniversary of his death a group of friends held the first Burns supper in the cottage where he was born. The tradition of Burns suppers grew from there, though they are now held on the anniversary of his birth, 25 January.

The cottage in which he lived has been fully restored and visitors to the Burns Heritage Park are given the opportunity to understand his humble background and to view the scenery that instilled in him a love of the Scottish landscape and culture. There is an impressive collection of authentic artefacts and a chance to enjoy some of his most famous works, such as *Tam 'O Shanter* brought to life.

*opposite The humble entrance to Burns' Cottage.*

# Down House

Down House in Kent was the home in which the pioneering naturalist Charles Darwin formulated the theories and carried out the experiments that would lead to his ground-breaking work, *The Origin of Species by Means of Natural Selection.*

As a theology student at Cambridge University, Darwin had already shown a strong interest in natural history. As a result, he was taken on board HMS *Beagle* as the ship's naturalist on a five-year-long trip to Patagonia, during which he also visited Tenerife, the Cape Verde Islands, Brazil and, most famously, the Galapagos Islands. It was during this trip that Darwin's

**Down House**
**Downe**
**Bromley**
**Kent**
**BR6 7JT**

**Tel 01689 859119**
**www.english-heritage.org.uk**

**Opening**
Down House is open from March – December, Wednesday – Sunday. For further information please see the website.

**Getting There**
The house is 4 miles from Orpington train station. Buses run from Orpington and from Bromley North and South stations.

**Concessions**
Children under 16
Families
Over 60s
Pre-booked groups (11 or more)
Students
Unemployed

**Facilities**

ideas about evolution began to take shape. He returned to England in 1836.

Six years later, he moved with his family to Down House. The house dates from the late eighteenth century. Both the house and gardens were improved and adapted, to become both a family home and a place for Darwin to carry out his field studies. High flint walls were built and apple-trees planted. Darwin used the gardens and outbuildings to grow and observe many plant species and breed pigeons. He had a particular interest in orchids and insectivorous plants,

which he cultivated in greenhouses. His definitive book was published in 1859. Twelve years later, it was followed by the work applying his theories to humans, *The Descent of Man*. When not studying or writing, Darwin lived the life of a country gentleman.

During his long voyage with the *Beagle*, he had contracted an illness which left him a semi-invalid for much of his life. Darwin died at Down House in 1882. The house and gardens have been restored and can be seen much as they were in his time, along with a range of exhibitions about his life and work.

**SPECIAL FEATURE**
The 'sandpath' or 'thinking path' was created in 1846. A circular walk planted with native trees, Darwin would mark off his laps around it with flints.

*above Down House.*

# The Brontë Parsonage

Brontë devotees will be in heaven in the Brontë parsonage, home to the most famous literary family, as it evokes so much of the spirit and character of the Brontës' world. The parsonage and its surrounding countryside provided Charlotte, Emily and Anne with the inspiration for what have become some of the best loved books in the English language.

The girl's father, Patrick Brontë, struggled from a humble background in Ireland to Cambridge University. He appreciated the value of education and fostered his children's interest in art, literature, music and politics. He was appointed incumbent at Haworth in 1820 and moved his wife and six children there. Haworth remained their home for the rest of their lives. The Museum now there, has preserved all aspects of the parsonage offering a riveting insight into the lives of the Brontë sisters.

The sisters worked as teachers and governesses, but preferred to be at home where they were always writing. The dining room is where they did most of their writing and planning. It was their habit to walk around the table until 11 o'clock in the evening, reading and discussing their ideas. After Emily and Anne died, a servant reported that Charlotte walked in solitude, unable to sleep without this nightly ritual.

Patrick Brontë was not told that Charlotte had written a book until she visited him in his study and produced a copy of the newly published *Jane Eyre*. He announced, 'Children, Charlotte has been writing a book and I think it is a better one than I had expected.'

In the kitchen the Brontë children would listen to Tabby their servant tell them stories of life on the moors, and upstairs is the room Charlotte occupied with her husband and later where she died. A tour reveals the smallest details of their lives and tells the fascinating tale of this close-knit family.

*opposite The Brontë Parsonage seen from the churchyard.*

**The Brontë Parsonage Museum
Church Street
Haworth, Keighley
West Yorkshire
BD22 8DR**

**Tel 01535 642323
www.bronte.info**

**Opening**
Daily except for 24–27 December and 2–31 January.

**Getting There**
Haworth is in West Yorkshire, 8 miles west of Bradford. Trains and coaches run to Leeds, a local train runs to Keighley and local buses from Keighley to Haworth.

**Concessions**
Children 5–16; under 5s free
Families, Over 60s,
Students, Unemployed

**Facilities**

**INTERESTING FACT**
The Brontë sisters attended The Clergy Daughter's School, the inspiration for Lowood school in *Jane Eyre*. Maria and Elizabeth Brontë died after falling ill there.

# Eltham Palace

There was a moated manor on the site of Eltham Palace, probably hundreds of years before it was acquired by Edward II in 1305. It became a royal palace for hundreds more years, with Edward IV adding the Great Hall with its oak hammerbeam roof in the 1470s. Henry VIII grew up here. But, like many great houses, Eltham Palace was neglected after the Civil War and for a period the Great Hall was used as a barn.

In 1933, Stephen and Virginia Courtauld took out a long lease on the site and set about transforming it into a definitive homage to Art Deco. Sir Stephen was the younger brother of Samuel, the industrialist, art collector and founder of the Courtauld Institute. Family wealth meant that finance was not a bar to the couple's imagination as they re-modelled Eltham, with the help of architects John Seeley and Paul Paget, and the fashionable interior designer Peter Malacrida.

Most of the old buildings were removed, but the Great Hall was preserved. Next to it, the Courtaulds used brick and Slipsham stone to construct an opulent house in two wings, joined by a semicircle of arches and columns. Inside, the walls are veneered in lacquered wood – the bird's-eye maple in the dining-room is especially eye-catching – echoing the interior of an ocean liner, a popular theme in the 1930s. There are shiny surfaces that wink in the light; the ceiling of the dining room is decorated with aluminium leaf. Light is diffused into the triangular entrance hall through a dome inset with glass.

There are even heated quarters for the Courtaulds' pet ring-tailed lemur!

Practicality was not ignored. There is a centralized vacuum system, built-in audio network throughout

**Eltham Palace**
**Greenwich**
**London**
**SE9 5QE**

**Tel 0208 294 2548**
**www.english-heritage.org.uk/**
**elthampalace**

**Opening**
The palace is open from Sunday – Wednesday most of the year, but closed from 24 December to 2 February. Further opening times available from the website.

**Getting There**
Eltham Palace is off Court Road. Eltham and Mottingham Junction stations are both half a mile away. There are several buses from surrounding areas and central London.

**Concessions**
Children 5–16 years
Families
Over-60s
Pre-booked groups (11 or more)
Students
Unemployed

**Facilities**

the house, concealed lighting and underfloor heating. Outside, the gardens boast a pergola, a loggia and rose plantations.

*opposite An interior shot of Eltham Palace.*

> **SPECIAL FEATURE**
> In Virginia's bathroom, a marble bath is surrounded by walls of onyx and tiny gold mosaic tiles. There are gold-plated bespoke taps and a statue of the goddess Psyche.

# Belton House

The Brownlow family had already owned land in the area for a hundred years when Sir John Brownlow decided to use some of the family fortune to build Belton House. The building took place between 1685 and 1689. The architect is not known for certain, though it is likely that William Winde and William Stanton were largely responsible for the design. Whoever its creators were, Belton is regarded as a particularly fine example of the style of architecture known as 'Carolean', after Charles II. It is symmetrical and relatively modest, and not an elaborate palace. Inevitably, succeeding generations made alterations. But many features were restored to their original state under the third Earl Brownlow in the nineteenth century.

The entrance hall offers a dramatic welcome with its chequerboard marble floor, family portraits and intricate limewood carvings. Beyond the hall, the salon is even more imposing. Giltwood mirrors are surrounded by more carving and there are full-length

portraits, including a likeness of Sir John Brownlow, Belton's builder, his wife and two of their five daughters, one of whom died of smallpox on the eve of her wedding. The tapestry room was remodelled in 1890 around the eighteenth-century tapestries made at the famous Mortlake factory. The Chinese room is hung with eighteenth-century Chinese wallpaper showing birds, butterflies and Chinese characters; the joinery in the room is painted to imitate bamboo. The Hondecoeter room is named after three vast oil paintings by the artist fitted into the panelling. The bedrooms contain beautifully made beds; the example in the blue bedroom is over 16 foot high.

In the chapel there is an awe-inspiring carved reredos, which was painted to look like marble at the end of the nineteenth century.

The gardens and park spread over a thousand acres, with the straight drive from the entrance steps to the Lion Gates being a mile long. The gardens were largely created in the nineteenth century. There is a Dutch and an Italian garden, an orangery, statues and a dramatic sundial.

*opposite Belton House, from the mile-long driveway.*

**Belton House
Grantham
Lincolnshire, NG32 2LS**

Tel 01476 566116
www.nationaltrust.org.uk

**Getting There**
Belton House is 3 miles north-east of Grantham, where there is a station. Buses run from Grantham, Lincoln and Sleaford.

**Concessions**
Children 5–15 years; under 5s free
Families
Groups

**Facilities**

# Woolsthorpe Manor

Woolsthorpe Manor near Grantham was the birthplace of the great scientist Sir Isaac Newton. He was born here on 25 December 1642, two months after the death of his father, a prosperous yeoman farmer. His mother went on to remarry and raise another family nearby while Newton grew up at this house with his grandmother. His intellectual ability was clearly evident. With little company, he would spend his time trying to calculate wind speed, making sundials or getting to grips with astronomy. In 1661, his family decided that he should not be consigned to a rustic life, and he went to study at Cambridge.

In 1665 the university was closed for two years by the Plague and Newton returned to Woolsthorpe. This was the period he described later as his 'prime' since during this time he arrived at three central concepts: the principle of differential calculus and the composition of white light. And by tradition, it was in the orchard at Woolsthorpe that Newton saw an apple fall and started on the train of thought that lead to his formulation of the Law of Gravitation.

After this interlude, however, and having become a professor at Cambridge at the age of twenty-six, he preferred to work in his laboratory, barely returning to Woolsthorpe, even when he inherited the house on his mother's death. On his own death in 1727, it passed to other farming families. It was finally acquired by the Royal Society, who in turn gave it to the National Trust to be restored and refurbished as a memorial to Newton.

The building itself, which was bought by Newton's grandfather, is a typical early seventeenth century manor house. It is laid out in a T-shape and has mullioned windows. The large upper room has a wainscot partition believed to have been installed by Newton for greater peace and quiet. Woolsthorpe Manor has been furnished with typical contemporary furnishings. There is still an apple orchard in front of the house.

*opposite The garden at Woolsthorpe Manor where Newton developed many of his theories.*

---

**Woolsthorpe Manor**
**23 Newton Way**
**Woolsthorpe-by-Colsterworth**
**Grantham**
**Lincolnshire, NG33 5NR**

**Tel 01476 860338**
**www.nationaltrust.org.uk**

**Opening**
Open Wednesdays to Sundays from March to September. Then weekends only until the end of October. Check website for further opening times.

**Getting There**
Woolsthorpe is 7 miles south of Grantham, where there is a train station. Buses run from Grantham.

**Concessions**
Children 3–15 years; under 3s free
Families
Groups

**Facilities**

---

**SPECIAL FEATURE**
An early edition of Newton's *Principia Mathematica* is on display. One of the most important books ever written, it laid the foundation for modern physics.

# Wilberforce House

**William Wilberforce's name will always be associated with the abolition of slavery in the British Empire.**

He was born on 24 August 1759 in Hull, the son of a wealthy merchant. He studied at Cambridge, where he made friends with the future prime minister, William Pitt the Younger. He and Pitt both entered parliament in 1780, Wilberforce as MP for Hull. He acquired a reputation for radicalism, that he later found embarrassing, by advocating parliamentary reform and Roman Catholic emancipation. He also led something of a wild life. This changed from 1784, when he became an evangelical Christian and joined a group called the Clapham Sect. His new Christian faith prompted an interest in social reform, particularly the improvement of factory conditions. In 1802 he organised the Society for the Suppression of Vice; he was also active in the Association for Better Observance of Sunday, which aimed to provide all children with education in reading and religion. His

interests were not limited to the welfare of people – he also had a close involvement with the RSPCA.

It is his role in ending slavery for which he is best known, however the abolitionist Thomas Clarkson was an important influence: he was already campaigning for an end to the practice of taking slaves from Africa to the Caribbean in British ships. Wilberforce lobbied with Clarkson for eighteen years, as did many members of the Clapham Sect. Trade in slaves was abolished in 1807. In 1833 an act was passed freeing all slaves in the Empire. Wilberforce died shortly afterwards, and was buried near Pitt in Westminster Abbey.

Wilberforce was born in this house in Hull. He lived there as a child, and later as an adult when he was an MP. Recently refurbished, it is a fascinating illustration of his life and work.

*opposite The statue of William Wilberforce in the garden of Wilberforce House.*

**Wilberforce House Museum**
**23–25 High Street**
**Hull, HU1 1NQ**

**Tel 01482 300300**
**www.hullcc.gov.uk**

**Opening**
The house is open daily.

**Getting There**
In the centre of Hull. Served by trains and local buses.

**Concessions**
Admission to the house and museum is free.

**Facilities**

# Sandringham House

The site of Sandringham House has been occupied since Elizabethan times. Sandringham Hall was built by the architect Cornish Henley in 1771 and modified by succeeding owners during the nineteenth century. It came into the possession of the royal family in 1862 when, at his request, Queen Victoria bought it for her eldest son, Albert Edward, the Prince of Wales – later Edward VII. The estate cost £220,000, furnishings included. The Prince of Wales took up residence in 1863 with his new wife, Princess Alexandra of Denmark.

The couple made a large number of adjustments and improvements to the estate. They built roads, rebuilt cottages and added a new garden wall. But by 1865 it had become clear that the existing house wasn't suited to its purpose as a principal royal residence. It was decided to knock it down and start from scratch and the architect A.J. Humbert was engaged for the job. The new house, built in red brick, was finished late in 1870, a country house for a family, rather than a palace.

The Prince of Wales was a devotee of shooting. In order to make more of daylight hours in winter to pursue his hobby, he invented 'Sandringham Time'; all the clocks in the house were set half an hour early. The tradition was maintained until Edward VIII abolished it in 1936.

The eldest son of the Prince of Wales, the Duke of Clarence, died of severe flu at Sandringham in 1892. This left his brother, George, as heir to the throne after his father. Prince George married his brother's fiancée, May of Teck, and they moved into a house on the estate which came to be known as York Cottage. The estate was passed down the generations

and saw its share of historic events. In 1932 George V made the first Christmas broadcast to the empire, live from the 'business room'. And in February 1952, George VI, who had been born in York Cottage, died at Sandringham.

*opposite and overleaf The nineteenth-century Sandringham House.*

**Sandringham House**
**Sandringham**
**Norfolk, PE35 6EN**

**Tel 01553 612908**
**www.sandringhamestate.co.uk**

**Opening**
The house is open daily from April to October. Further information from website or by phone.

**Getting There**
Sandringham is 6 miles north-east of King's Lynn. Trains run to King's Lynn and there are bus services from the town.

**Concessions**
Children 5–15 years; under 5s free
Disabled and carers
Families
Groups (20 or more, pre-booked)
Over 60s
Students

**Facilities**

**SPECIAL FEATURE**
The iron Norwich Gates were designed by Thomas Jekyll. They were a wedding gift to the future Edward VII and Queen Alexandra from the people of that city.

# Erddig

**The house at Erddig is both home to a significant collection of furniture and art, and also a remarkable record of the relationship between the owning family and their staff over two centuries.**

The first house, an austere square building by Thomas Webb, was finished in 1687. It was sold to the Master of Chancery, John Meller, in 1716. He furnished and enlarged the house, adding two wings on either side of the central block, but the exterior of Erddig was still rather forbidding. Inside, it was a different story. Meller collected items from leading London craftsmen. There are silver and walnut chairs, ornate mirrors, brightly coloured detailing and large tapestries. The state bed was also transported from London. The collection was continued by Meller's great-nephew, Philip Yorke I, who was a keen antiquarian with an interest in oriental art. He created the library and decorated rooms with Chinese wallpaper and paintings. He also re-faced the west front, which had been damaged by constant battering by the elements.

The house is a reminder of the high regard the Yorke family had for their staff. There are more portraits of servants than of the family. The basement passage contains photographs and there are painted portraits from the eighteenth century in the servants' hall. From the living and working environments provided, it seems that staff at Erdigg were exceptionally well looked after. There were certainly plenty of them; up to thirty workmen were employed at a time to look after the estate alone. There was a bakehouse, a sawmill, a smithy and a joiner's shop. This was very much a working community.

Philip Yorke I's anitiquarian interests also led him to preserve the garden in its old-fashioned style. He employed William Emes to landscape the park – which included the installation of the circular waterfall called the 'Cup and Saucer' and the hanging beech woods — but retained the formal layout nearer the house, much of which already dated back fifty years.

*opposite The house and gardens at Erddig.*

---

**Erddig
Wrexham
LL13 0YT**

**Tel 01978 355314
www.nationaltrust.org.uk**

**Opening**
House open from March to October, Saturdays to Wednesdays. Garden open March to December, also Saturdays to Wednesdays. Please check the website for further details.

**Getting There**
Erddig is 2 miles south of Wrexham. It is signposted off the A525 and the A483. Trains run to Wrexham Central and Wrexham General. From buses, alight at Felin Puleston and walk 1 mile through the country park.

**Concessions**
Children 3–16 years; under 3s free
Families (2 adults, 3 children)
Groups (15 or more)

**Facilities**

**SPECIAL FEATURE**
Some of the servants are portrayed in old age. The picture of Edward Prince, a carpenter, shows him aged 75, still looking strong and healthy.

# Hardwick Hall

'Hardwick Hall, more glass than wall' was the creation of Elizabeth Shrewsbury, better known to history as Bess of Hardwick, who was nearly seventy years old when work started on the house in 1590. The old saying about the Hall arose from its unique, huge windows, taller on each successive storey, making the house look like a giant lantern.

Bess, who had become richer with each of her four marriages, set out to build a house fit for royalty. It has six towers, pulling the eye to the roof, where Bess's initials are drawn in stone against the skyline. Inside, a broad stone staircase winds between floors with rooms full of furniture, paintings and tapestries, most from the Elizabethan period, but some dating from the early nineteenth century, when they were added by Bess's descendant, the 6th Duke of Devonshire. More than eighty paintings hang in the long gallery, many of them portraits of royalty and nobility from Bess's own time, illustrating her connections and influence. The High Great Chamber on the third floor, intended expressly for receiving such important guests, was designed around massive tapestries bought in 1587 and still hanging there today. The plaster frieze above them shows the goddess Diana and her attendants. It was meant as a tribute to Queen Elizabeth I – although Bess was disappointed in her hope that the Queen would visit.

Outside there are formal gardens, with walks edged by yew and hornbeam trees. A herb garden is stocked with medicinal plants used by the Elizabethans. A small banqueting house was used as a smoking-room by the 6th Duke's private orchestra, who weren't allowed to smoke in the Hall. The surrounding estate has two distinct landscapes: to the back of the house, formal lawns; to the front, hillier land, grazed by rare breeds of cattle and sheep. There are also the remains of the Old Hall, where Bess was born.

*opposite Sunset at Hardwick Hall.*

**Hardwick Hall
Doe Lea
Chesterfield
Derbyshire
S44 5QJ**

Tel 01246 850430
www.nationaltrust.org.uk

**Opening**
The Hall is open Wednesday, Thursday, Saturday and Sunday, March – October. The garden is open from Wednesday – Sunday on the same dates. The Park is open daily throughout the year. For further opening times, please telephone or see the website.

**Getting There**
Hardwick Hall is 6 miles west of Mansfield and 9 miles south-east of Chesterfield. Trains call at Chesterfield. Buses run from Chesterfield, Sheffield and Nottingham.

**Concessions**
Children under 15 years
Families
Pre-booked groups

**Facilities**

**SPECIAL FEATURE**
The eglantine table in the High Great Chamber was probably made for Bess's marriage to the Earl of Shrewsbury in 1568 and features a mosaic of board games.

# Syon Park

Syon Park boasts perhaps the finest Robert Adam interior in the country. It is the last ducal residence complete with country estate in Greater London. The house has magnificent state and private apartments and the Great Conservatory is set in 200 acres of gardens.

Originally the site of a medieval abbey, Syon was named after Mount Zion in the Holy Land. The abbey was dissolved by Henry VIII in 1539 when it became crown property. It was given to the Duke of Somerset, the Lord Protector to Edward VI and he built Syon House in the Italian Renaissance style. The house was acquired by John Dudley, whose son married Lady Jane Grey; it was at Syon that she was formally offered the crown.

The first Duke of Northumberland redesigned the estate in the 1760s and employed Robert Adam to remodel the interior of Syon House in neoclassical style. The famous Great Hall is based on a Roman basilica. Adam's aim was to create a palace of Graeco-Roman splendour. The cool pale stucco tones are only broken by the black and white marble floor, which repeats the pattern on the ceiling. The ante room, by contrast, is richly decorated with a riot of coloured marble and gilded statues of gods, supported on green marble columns and standing on a beautiful scagliola floor. The state dining room has a clean white and gold interior decorated with stucco, sculpture and painting, which would not, according to Adam, retain the smell of food.

The red drawing room has an incredible painted ceiling by Cipriani with 239 painted medallions. The walls are hung with crimson silk and display a series of paintings of the Stuart royal family.

Lancelot 'Capability' Brown was employed to landscape the grounds, which contain an extensive collection of rare trees and plants and a beautiful lake in which terrapins can be found.

Syon Park
Brentford
Middlesex
TW8 8JF

Tel 020 8560 0881
www.syonpark.co.uk

**Opening**
The house is open from mid-March to the end of October on Wednesdays, Thursdays and Sundays, and some Bank holidays; please check the website for details. The gardens are open daily from March to October and at weekends only from November to February.

**Getting There**
Syon Park is 10 miles from Central London and easily accessible by car. The nearest train station is Kew Bridge and the nearest Underground station is Gunnersbury, and number 237 and 267 buses run from these stations.

**Concessions**
Children 5–16 years; under 5s free
Families
Over 60s

**Facilities**

**INTERESTING FACT**
In 1587 King Henry VIII's coffin was brought to Syon en route to Windsor for burial. It burst open in the night and dogs were found licking the remains.

*opposite Inside the Great Conservatory, Syon Park.*

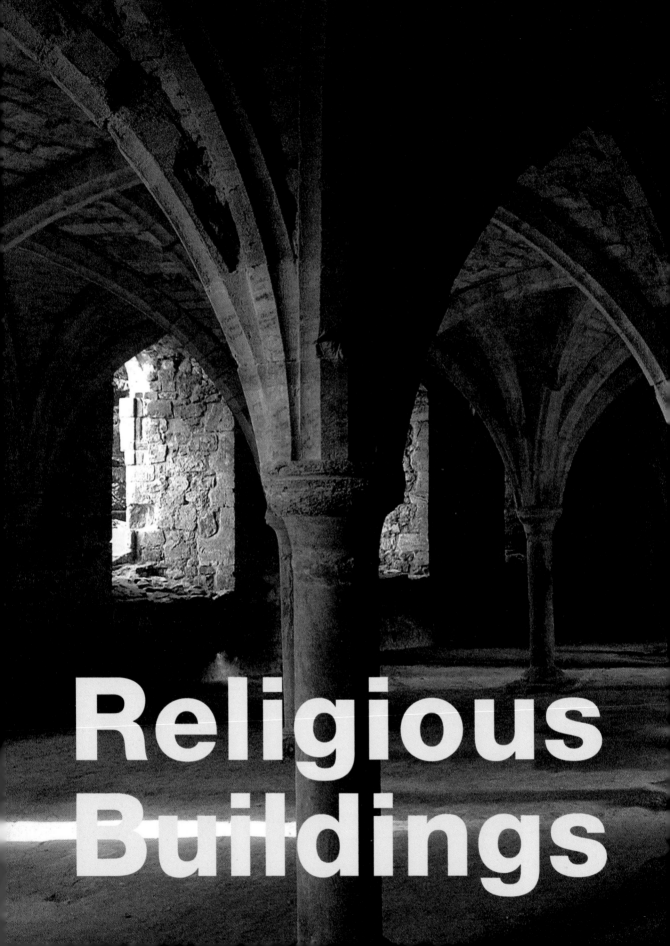

# Religious Buildings

# St David's Cathedral

Built on the site of St David's sixth century monastery, St David's Cathedral is the largest church in Wales and has been a place of pilgrimage and worship for centuries.

St David of Wales, or Dewi Sant, was the son of Sandde, Prince of Powys and Non, daughter of a chieftain of Menevia whose lands were on the peninsula where the city – in reality little more than a village – of St David's stands.

David became Abbot of St David's. He died on 1 March 589, now annually celebrated as St David's Day in Wales. It was not until the eleventh century however, when an account of his life was written by Rhygfarch that he became famous.

St David's was regularly raided by Vikings; a visitor in the eleventh century found an abandoned site and

**St David's Cathedral**
**St David's**
**Pembrokeshire**
**SA62 6RH**

**Tel 01437 720202**
**www.stdavidscathedral.org.uk**

**Opening**
Sightseeing daily from Monday to Saturday and Sunday afternoons. Special services or events may close the cathedral at short notice, so please check the website before visiting.

**Getting There**
Trains run from London Paddington to the nearest station at Haverfordwest. Buses run from here to St David's.

**Concessions**
Entry is free, donations are welcome.

**Facilities**

**INTERESTING FACT**
Look for the tomb of Edmund Tudor, founder of the Tudor dynasty and the Abraham Stone, an eleventh century Celtic grave marker.

St David's tomb lost among undergrowth and stripped of precious metals. A new shrine was constructed in 1275, although the ruins of the original shrine have been preserved. The relics of St David and St Justinian were kept in a portable shrine, but were confiscated by Bishop Barlow during the Reformation, in order to discourage idolatry.

The nave is the oldest part of the building and was constructed in the twelfth century by Bishop Peter de Leia and Giraldus de Barri; both were excused from the Third Crusade in order to complete the cathedral. In 1120 Pope Calixtus recognised St David and declared that two pilgrimages to St David's were equivalent to one to Rome and three were equal to one pilgrimage to Jerusalem. Inadequate foundations and the effects of a thirteenth-century earthquake have caused the walls at the west end of the nave to lean outwards, necessitating the magnificent oak ceilings.

Rebuilding programmes were undertaken by John Nash in the eighteenth century and Sir Gilbert Scott in the nineteenth century. Neither could change the fact that the floor rises fourteen feet between the West Door to the High Altar – legend maintains that the slope takes the congregation closer to heaven. The Chapel of Edward the Confessor was re-roofed in the twentieth century, parliamentary soldiers having stripped the lead in 1648.

*opposite and overleaf* Views of St David's Cathedral.

# Westminster Abbey

Westminster Abbey is a standing tribute to the architectural masters of the thirteenth through to the sixteenth centuries. It has been the backdrop for every coronation since 1066, bar two (Edward V and Edward VIII), and has witnessed countless other great royal occasions. It contains the shrine of Edward the Confessor, the tombs of many kings and queens and those of poets, musicians, scientists, statesmen and soldiers.

Edward the Confessor oversaw the building of Westminster Abbey, although when his new church was consecrated on 28 December 1065, the king was too ill to attend; he died a few days later and

**Westminster Abbey**
**Broad Sanctuary**
**London**
**SW1P 3PA**

**Tel 020 7222 5152**
**www.westminster-abbey.org**

**Opening**
Sightseeing daily from Monday to Saturday. Special services or events may close the abbey at short notice; please check the website before visiting.

**Getting There**
Westminster Abbey is in the heart of London in Parliament Square, opposite the Houses of Parliament. The nearest Underground stations are St James's Park and Westminster.

**Concessions**
Children 11–16; under 11s free
Families
Over 60s, Students

**Facilities**

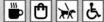

> **INTERESTING FACT**
> Many of Britain's greatest poets are buried in Poet's Corner. However, poet Ben Jonson 1574–1637, was buried upright in the nave, to save precious floor space.

was entombed in front of the High Altar. Edward's abbey survived two more centuries, witnessing the coronation of William the Conqueror on Christmas Day 1066 and the moving of Edward's body to a new tomb after his canonization in 1161.

In the mid-thirteenth century Henry III decided to rebuild the abbey and create an immense gothic structure. It was designed to be both a monastery and a place of worship, as well as a suitable venue for coronations and royal burials. Work, which halted on his death, then continued for another 250 years. Many monarchs are buried around Edward the Confessor's shrine, notably Henry III, Edward I, Eleanor of Castile, Edward III, Richard II and Henry V. Over 3000 people are buried in the abbey including the Unknown Soldier. Mary I, Elizabeth I, James I and Charles II all reside here along with such luminaries as Charles Dickens, Charles Darwin and Geoffrey Chaucer.

Henry VII built the Lady Chapel, which has an extraordinary fan-vaulted roof. Two centuries later Sir Christopher Wren and Nicholas Hawksmoor designed the western towers.

The abbey has hosted many royal weddings, including that of Albert Duke of York, later King George VI to Elizabeth Bowes-Lyon who laid her bouquet on the tomb of the Unknown Soldier, which has since become a royal tradition.

*opposite Westminster Abbey seen from the Dean's Yard.*

# Ely Cathedral

Ely Cathedral was essentially created by one woman. Etheldreda was a Saxon princess born at Exning, near Newmarket, in 630. She was married twice, but was convinced that she was really destined for the religious life. Her first husband bequeathed her the Isle of Ely. Her second husband, Eegrfrid, allowed their marriage to be dissolved and Etheldreda fled to Ely where she founded a monastery for both monks and nuns. She was installed as the first Abbess.

Etheldreda died in 679 of a throat tumour, which she believed was a punishment for wearing jewelled necklaces in earlier life. Twenty years later, her body was moved from the monastery grounds into the Saxon church on the site in which a shrine to her was created. The historian Bede records that Etheldreda's body was seen to be exceptionally well preserved and the tumour healed.

Etheldreda's monastery flourished until it and much of the city of Ely were destroyed in Danish invasions at the end of the ninth century. In 970, it was refounded as a Benedictine community.

Work on the present building began at the end of the eleventh century under Abbot Simeon. In 1109 what had been started as a new monastery church became a cathedral when the diocese of Ely was carved out of the diocese of Lincoln. The Anglo-Saxon church was demolished, but many of its relics were moved to the new cathedral. Not all principles of engineering were fully understood then; Simeon's tower fell down in 1322, destroying the choir. It was replaced by a beautiful octagonal tower, culminating in a wooden lantern which is the only Gothic dome in existence.

Etheldreda's shrine was destroyed in the Dissolution of the monasteries in 1539, along with statues, carving and stained glass. The cathedral was refounded in 1541, with the last prior of the monastery as the first dean of the cathedral.

In the late 1830s the final stage of restoration was completed under Dean George Peacock and the celebrated architect George Gilbert Scott.

*opposite* The south-west transept of Ely Cathedral.

---

**Ely Cathedral**
**Cambridgeshire**
**CB7 4DL**

**Tel 01353 667735**
**www.cathedral.ely.anglican.org**

**Opening**
Daily, with some restrictions on Sundays and holy days. Details by phone or website.

**Getting There**
The cathedral is in the centre of the city. Trains call at Ely from London (King's Cross or Liverpool Street), Cambridge, Peterborough, Norwich and Stansted Airport.

**Concessions**
Entry is free, but donations are welcomed.

**Facilities**

---

**SPECIAL FEATURE**
The Lady Chapel is the largest attached to a British cathedral. It was built from 1321 in the Decorated style and was badly defaced during the Reformation.

# Fountains Abbey

In 1132 a dispute broke out among the monks at the Benedictine abbey of St Mary's, in York, resulting in the departure of a small group who were seeking a stricter adherence to the rules of monastic life. They were taken under the wing of Thurstan, Archbishop of York. He settled them on land in the Skell River valley, a suitably remote position, but where they would have access to building materials, shelter and running water. The monks wrote to Bernard at the Cistercian Abbey of Clairvaux in France, seeking affiliation with his strict order of White Monks. In 1135, they were formally accepted into the Cistercian family.

Despite their ideal location, the early years were hard. The community was on the point of disbanding when

**Fountains Abbey**
**Ripon**
**North Yorkshire**
**HD4 3DY**

**Tel 01765 608888**
**www.nationaltrust.org.uk**

**Opening**
Open daily. Closed on Fridays from November to March.

**Getting There**
The Abbey is 4 miles west of Ripon. Buses run from York, Wakefield, Leeds and Harrogate, all of which have train connections.

**Concessions**
Children 5–15 years; under 5s free
Families
Groups (15 or more)

**Facilities**

its fortunes were changed by the arrival of several wealthy recruits, including Hugh, the former Dean of York. The monastery flourished and by the end of the twelfth century it owned land in over two hundred locations and was playing an important role in ecclestical and even political affairs.

Building began in 1132. Originally the abbey would have been a simple complex, built on strict Cistercian principles. But over the centuries it was added to and altered. The church, dedicated to the Virgin Mary like all Cistercian monastery churches, was built to the north of the river. It wasn't until around 1500, under Abbot

Huby, that it received its impressive tower, in an odd position at the north end of the transept. An equally impressive vaulted cellarium, over 300 feet long, spans the river. On one floor it would have had cellars and storerooms; above was the dormitory for the lay brothers whose labour was central to Cistercian life.

During the Dissolution of the monasteries, Fountains and about 500 acres was sold to Sir Richard Gresham, whose son founded the London Stock Exchange. Eventually, in 1768, it came to William Aislabie, who set about preserving the abbey and creating idyllic surroundings for it.

**SPECIAL FEATURE**
The abbey church has an extra transept at the eastern end of the presbytery. This highly unusual feature is known as the Chapel of the Nine Altars.

*above The remains at Fountains Abbey.*

# St Paul's Cathedral

St Paul's Cathedral – Christopher Wren's impressive masterpiece – is a distinctive feature of the London skyline. A cathedral dedicated to St Paul has overlooked the City of London since 604 AD, a reminder to this commercial centre of activity of the importance of the more spiritual side of life. The current cathedral is the fourth to occupy the site after its predecessor was destroyed in the Great Fire of London in 1666. Wren oversaw the construction of the cathedral between 1675 and 1710.

St Paul's is built in the shape of a cross with the dome crowning the intersection of the arms. The dome is one of the largest in the world, some 111.3 metres high; it weighs approximately 65,000 tonnes and is supported by eight pillars. While the dome and the galleries were being built Wren was hauled up in a basket once a week to inspect the works; he was seventy-six by the time it was completed. The whispering gallery runs around the dome 259 steps above ground level. It is so called because a whisper against the wall on one side is audible all the way round on the other. The ball and cross topping the dome stand twenty-three feet high and weigh approximately seven tonnes.

The 1695 organ on which Mendelssohn once played is still in use. The organ case, designed by Grinling Gibbons, is one of the cathedral's greatest artefacts and is the third largest in the UK.

On the cathedral floor there are memorials to Wellington, Nelson, J.M.W. Turner, and an effigy to the seventeenth-century metaphysical poet John Donne, who was a dean of the cathedral. Many other prominent men are interred in the crypt, including the architect himself Christopher Wren, the painters John Everett Millais and Joshua Reynolds, the composer Sir Arthur Sullivan (of Gilbert and Sullivan), Admiral Lord Nelson and the Iron Duke Wellington.

*opposite St Paul's Cathedral.*

---

**St Paul's Cathedral**
**St Paul's Churchyard**
**London**
**EC4M 8AD**

**Tel 0207 236 4128**
**www.stpauls.co.uk**

**Opening**
Sightseeing daily from Monday to Saturday. Special services or events may close the cathedral at short notice, please check the website before visiting.

**Getting There**
The nearest Underground station is St Paul's, which is a five minute walk from the cathedral. Blackfriars and Mansion House stations are also close. The 4, 11, 115, 23, 26 and 100 buses stop outside St Paul's.

**Concessions**
Children 7–16 years; under 7s free
Families
Over 60s
Students

**Facilities**

---

**INTERESTING FACT**

Nelson lies in the crypt in a sarcophagus made for Cardinal Wolsey. The body was preserved on the journey from Trafalgar in a barrel filled with French Brandy.

# Liverpool Cathedral

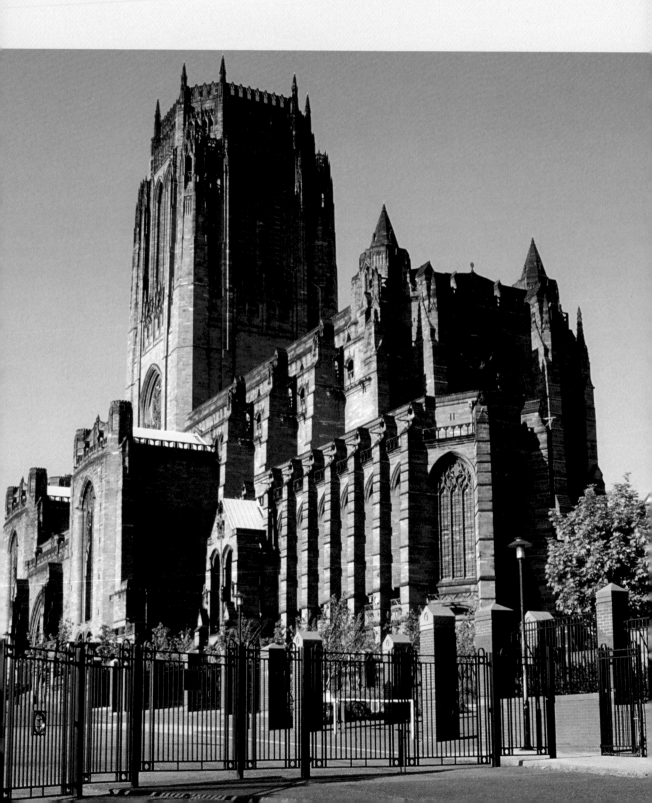

Liverpool Cathedral is a record breaker; it is the largest cathedral in Britain and the fifth largest in the world. It has the highest and widest Gothic arches in the world and the highest and heaviest peal of bells in the world. Sir John Betjeman wrote, 'This is one of the great buildings of the world...the impression of vastness, strength and height no words can describe.'

In 1880 John Ryle was appointed the first Bishop of Liverpool; he was installed in St Peters' Church, a building generally regarded as hideous. This goes some way to explaining why, in 1901, the city approved the decision to build a more impressive cathedral.

A twenty-two-year old architect, Giles Gilbert Scott, won an open competition to design it. He and George Bodley were appointed joint architects and the foundation stone was laid by Edward VII in 1904. The Lady Chapel was dedicated in 1910, and the main part of the cathedral was consecrated in July 1924, exactly twenty years on from the laying of the foundation stone. Work on the cathedral continued, and during World War II the first services were held in the central space below the still-incomplete tower. The bridge and the first bay of the nave were completed in 1961 and final works completed in 1978. The cathedral's architecture is best described as awesome, and the tower offers panoramic views of the city.

Recently a £3 million visitor centre has been built. The 'Great Space' film and audio tour presents a unique way of exploring this twentieth-century architectural masterpiece, with an effective visual fly through and archive footage of the building process.

**INTERESTING FACT**
The cathedral choir was founded in 1910; Paul McCartney failed his audition in the 1950s, but has collaborated with it since, notably in his Liverpool Oratorio.

**Liverpool Cathedral**
**St James Mount**
**Liverpool**
**L1 7AZ**

Tel 0151 709 6271
www.liverpoolcathedral.org.uk

**Opening**
The cathedral is open daily to sightseers, but may be closed for special services, so please check the website for further details.

**Getting There**
The cathedral is a 25-minute uphill walk from the heart of the city. The nearest train station is Liverpool Lime Street and buses 82 and 82C run close to the cathedral. Drivers should follow signs for the city centre and cathedral at the end of the M62.

**Concessions**
Free entry, donations welcomed. Some facilities have an entrance fee.

**Facilities**

*opposite Liverpool's Anglican Cathedral.*

# Iona Abbey

**Home of saints and burial place of warrior kings, the island abbey of Iona has been an important Christian site for nearly 1,450 years and is one of Scotland's most sacred places.**

The abbey was founded in 563 by St Columba and a small band of brethren who made their way across the sea from Ireland. In the midst of dark and often violent times the abbey grew famous as a beacon of faith and learning. Tor an Aba, the little mound where Columba reputedly had his writing hut, can still be seen.

It remained the burial place of successive Scottish kings until Macbeth in 1057, but kings from Norway and France are also buried here, and at least two Irish kings retired to Iona to live out their final days.

Viking raiders took a terrible toll on the community with major raids in 795, 802, 806 and 825. But the monastery survived and flourished again under the

patronage of the Lords of the Isles, the Norse/Gaelic descendants of Somerled who built themselves a kingdom in the Hebrides. St Oran's Chapel was their burial place until the late fifteenth century, and the abbey still has a wonderful collection of grave slabs carved with effigies of once-powerful warlords.

Gradually the abbey buildings grew larger and more impressive, featuring a fine stone church, elegant cloisters, a bakery, infirmary and comfortable house for the abbot. The Reformation of 1560 brought the dissolution of the abbey and its buildings slowly fell into ruin. In the 1870s, however, the eighth Duke of Argyll hired celebrated architect Robert Rowand Anderson to consolidate the remains. Restoration took place in the early twentieth century and the abbey was reborn as a centre for Christian worship. The abbey is to this day a working religious community.

*opposite Iona Abbey and high cross on the island of Iona.*

**Iona Abbey**
**Isle of Iona**
**Argyllshire**
**PA76 6SQ**

**Tel 01681 700512**
**www.historic-scotland.gov.uk**

**Opening**
Daily except for Christmas Day and New Years Day.

**Getting There**
Iona Abbey can be reached by public ferry from Fionnphort on Mull. Check with Caledonian Macbrayne Hebriddean & Clyde Ferries at www.calmac.co.uk.

**Concessions**
Children 5–15 years; under 5s free
Over 60s

**Facilities**

# Lincoln Cathedral

**As a result of two disasters, the Cathedral Church of St Mary at Lincoln was built in three phases and has elements of both the Norman and early English styles.**

The first cathedral on the site was built by the Norman Bishop Remigius, who died just two days before its consecration in 1092. About fifty years later, most of the building was destroyed in a fire. Bishop Alexander rebuilt and expanded the cathedral, but in 1185 an earthquake caused substantial damage. The new bishop, Hugh, started a massively ambitious rebuild that continued long after his death. Beginning at the east end, he put in an apse and five small radiating chapels. Then the central nave was built, in Early English style. Lincoln was following the architectural developments of the time, using flying buttresses and ribbed vaulting, which strengthened the fabric of the building and allowed the insertion of larger windows and more elaborate decoration. Nonetheless, the central tower collapsed in the 1230s and had to be replaced.

During this period, St Hugh's choir, with its unusual, seemingly random vaulting, was built. Work also began on the two beautiful rose windows, The Bishop's Eye and The Dean's Eye.

Later rebuilds added choir aisles with unique double arcading, and an extension to the east end known as the Angel Choir, constructed in order to receive the tomb of Bishop St Hugh, which had become a place of pilgrimage. The western towers were raised and spires added, although these were eventually found to be unsafe and were removed in 1808. The central tower's spire blew down in 1549.

When Eleanor of Castile died in 1290, her husband King Edward I gave her a lavish funeral procession. She was embalmed, which involved removing her viscera (internal organs). Her tomb is at Westminster, but her viscera were taken to Lincoln and placed in a replica tomb. Although it is probably not the case, two prominent statues outside the cathedral are often said to represent Edward and Eleanor.

*opposite The imposing cathedral at Lincoln dwarves the surrounding houses.*

## SPECIAL FEATURE

The Lincoln Imp sits on a column in the Angel Choir, legs crossed and laughing. The story is that he was running amok in the cathedral when an angel turned him to stone.

**Lincoln Cathedral
Lincoln, LN2 1PX**

**Tel 01522 561600
www.lincolncathedral.com**

**Opening**
The cathedral is open daily, though there may be some restrictions on Sundays.

**Getting There**
The cathedral is in the heart of the city. Lincoln station has mainline connections at Newark. There are also connections to Birmingham, Nottingham, Grantham, Skegness and Grimsby.

**Concessions**
Children 5–15 years; under 5s free
Over 60s
Students

**Facilities**

# Lindisfarne

The priory at Lindisfarne, on Holy Island, was founded in the first half of the seventh century AD, when King Oswald of Northumbria invited Aidan to make the journey from his monastery at Iona. Northumbria was the most powerful of the Anglo-Saxon kingdoms, and Oswald's conversion to Christianity had a lasting significance. Aidan arrived on the island with twelve other monks.

Initially, the monstery was in the Irish style, comprising little more than some wooden huts. Once the monks had learned English they then followed a zealous life of missionary work and education, walking the lanes and talking with local people, and founding a school.

Although Aidan was the priory's founder, a later prior, Cuthbert, is perhaps better known. Cuthbert was the son of a well-to-do family from north Northumberland. He was trained in military skills

and probably took part in more than one skirmish, but after a religious vision, he entered the monstery at Melrose in Scotland, later moving to Lindisfarne as prior. It was possibly in his honour that his successor Eadfrith had the famous Lindisfarne Gospels made in the early years of the eighth century.

In 793, Viking raids began and the monks eventually fled. A monastery was later re-established on Lindisfarne, and remained until its dissolution under Henry VIII.

**Lindisfarne**
**Northumberland**
**TD15 2RX**

Tel 01289 389200
www.english-heritage.org.uk/
lindisfarnepriory

**Opening**
Open daily from February – end October. Then Saturday, Sunday and Monday until January.

**Getting There**
Berwick-upon-Tweed is 14 miles away. Trains run to Berwick and there are buses from there to Holy Island.

Note: The island and priory can only be reached across a causeway at low tide. Tide times are posted at both ends of the causeway and can also be obtained from Tourist Information (01289 330733).

**Concessions**
Children under 15 years; under 5s free
Families
Groups (15 or more)
Over 60s
Students
Unemployed

**Facilities**

**SPECIAL FEATURE**
The 'Rainbow Arch' is all that remains of the crossing-tower of the Norman nave. It was once just a vault-rib, but is now a powerful image of the priory's history.

*opposite* The ruins of Lindisfarne Priory.

# Glastonbury Abbey

Glastonbury Abbey occupies the site believed to be the location of the first Christian sanctuary in the world. Legend has it that it was visited by Joseph of Arimathea, St David and St Patrick. It is now a beautiful, romantic ruin in a very tranquil setting.

The Christian Saxons conquered Somerset in the seventh century. Their king, Ine of Wessex, is said to have erected a stone church there, the base of which forms the west end of the nave. The abbey was enlarged in the tenth century by St Dunstan and the Normans extended further. By 1068, when the Domesday Book was commissioned, Glastonbury was the richest monastery in England. It was destroyed by fire in 1184; the replacement was consecrated in 1213.

By the fourteenth century Glastonbury was second only to Westminster Abbey in terms of power and wealth, this at a time when there were more than 800 monasteries, nunneries and friaries in Britain. During the Dissolution of the Monasteries the crown seized all church buildings and by 1541 none was left; Glastonbury Abbey was one of its principal victims. It lay in a ruinous state until it was purchased in 1908 and preservation work begun.

Many legends are attached to Glastonbury; Jesus Christ and his great uncle Joseph of Arimathea are reputed to have built the first wattle-and-daub church at Glastonbury. After the Crucifixion Joseph returned to Britain and thrust his thorn staff into the ground. By morning it had taken root leaving a strange oriental thorn bush – the sacred Glastonbury Thorn which is still growing today.

Rumours abounded that King Arthur was buried at Glastonbury, though it was not known where. Monks excavated and unearthed a stone slab, underneath which was found a lead cross with the inscription, 'Here lies buried the renowned King Arthur in the Isle of Avalon.' Some smaller bones and a lock of hair were explained as belonging to Guinevere. In 1278 the bones were placed in a casket and transferred to a black marble tomb in the presence of Edward I. They remained there until the abbey was vandalised after the Dissolution, and have not been seen since.

*opposite The Abbey at Glastonbury.*

**Glastonbury Abbey**
**Magdalene Street**
**Glastonbury**
**Somerset**
**BA6 9EL**

**Tel 01458 832267**
**www.glastonburyabbey.com**

**Opening**
Open daily.

**Getting There**
Glastonbury Abbey is close to junction 23 of the M5. Trains run from London Paddington to Castle Cary, a taxi can take you on to the abbey. Alternatively travel by train to Bristol Temple Meads, Bath or Taunton and travel onward by bus.

**Concessions**
Children 5–15 years; under 5s free
Families
Over 60s
Students

**Facilities**

**INTERESTING FACT**
Legend states Joseph of Arimathea buried the Holy Grail at Glastonbury causing a spring to appear. The water from Chalice Well supposedly bestows eternal youth.

# Canterbury Cathedral

St Augustine arrived in England in 597, sent by Pope Gregory the Great. He was given a church at Canterbury, St Martin's, by the local king, Ethelbert, and around it he founded a Christian community. When the pope made him an archbishop, Augustine established Canterbury as his *cathedra*, or seat. The community formed around the cathedral became a formal organisation of Benedictine monks during the tenth century. The Saxons enlarged Augustine's cathedral, but after the Norman conquest Archbishop Lanfranc had it completely rebuilt in the Norman style between 1070 and 1077. A fire in 1174 led to major rebuilding work and the Cathedral was also extensively remodelled through the late fourteenth and fifteenth centuries.

The cathedral ceased to be the centre of a monastery when Henry VIII ordered the foundation closed in 1540. Responsibility for the cathedral upkeep and services passed to the dean and chapter. The building was damaged during the Civil War, when much of the stained glass was smashed by Puritans, who stabled their horses in the nave. This damage was repaired after the Restoration. In the early nineteenth century, the Norman north-west tower was found to be dangerous. It was demolished and replaced with a copy of the south-west tower, hence the cathedral's symmetrical appearance.

During World War II, remarkably little harm came to the cathedral, although the precincts were badly bombed.

The most famous incident in the history of Canterbury Cathedral was the murder of Archbishop Thomas á Becket in 1170. The Archbishop had transferred his allegiance from King Henry II to the pope, much to Henry's fury. The dispute escalated until it is believed four of Henry's knights heard him demand, 'Who will rid me of this meddlesome priest?' and took the job upon themselves. They duly murdered Becket during vespers in the Cathedral.

In 1173, Becket was canonised and the site of his murder became a place of pilgrimage. King Henry was one of the first pilgrims.

*opposite Canterbury Cathedral.*

---

**Canterbury Cathedral**
**Canterbury**
**Kent, CT1 2EH**

**Tel 01227 762862**
**www.canterbury-cathedral.org**

**Opening**
The cathedral is open daily throughout the year, although access is limited on Sundays and at certain other times. Details from the website or by phone.

**Getting There**
The cathedral is at the heart of the city of Canterbury, which is served by regular trains from London Victoria and London Charing Cross. There are also trains between Ashford and Canterbury West. There are plenty of buses to the city from local areas.

**Concessions**
Children
Over 60s
Some local residents
Students

**Facilities**

---

**SPECIAL FEATURE**
The crypt is the oldest remaining part of the cathedral and is the largest Romanesque crypt in Britain. Many of its decorative details have survived.

# Temple Church

The Temple Church is undoubtedly one of the most intriguing buildings in London. Its composite part-round, part-chancel structure is unmistakeable; it is one of only three round Norman churches in the country. The church's history is tied in with one of the most enigmatic organisations of the Middle Ages.

The church was built by the Knights Templar, an order of crusading monks founded to protect pilgrims on their way to and from Jerusalem. At this time, the late twelfth century, they were enormously powerful. Their new compound was part monastery, part military training base. The church was consecrated in 1185. Its shape was intended to recall the holiest place in the crusaders' world: the circular Church of the Holy Sepulchre in Jerusalem.

It was Henry III who caused the chancel section of the Temple Church to be added. Consecrated in 1240, it was a response to Henry's expressed desire to be buried in the church. He later changed his mind, and opted for Westminster Abbey.

The Templars became too wealthy for their own good and fell from favour until, in the fourteenth century, the order was abolished and control of the Temple came to the Knights Hospitaller. They rented it to two colleges of lawyers, who formed the Middle and Inner Temples, two of the Inns of Court. With one interruption, the Temple has been in the control of the Inns of Court ever since. It was during that interruption, with the Temple again under royal control,  that Shakespeare wrote *Henry VI, Part I*, setting a scene in the Temple garden in which a white and a red rose are plucked, supplying an irresistible fictional start to the Wars of the Roses. In 1608, James I granted the two Inns of Court use of the church in perpetuity.

After the Great Fire of London, the church, although undamaged, was restored by Sir Christopher Wren. Throughout all later changes and post-war restorations, it has stayed in regular use.

*opposite Temple Church (c1185) located off Fleet Street.*

**Temple Church**
**London, EC4Y 7BB**

**Tel 020 7353 3470**
**www.templechurch.com**

**Opening**
The church is generally open Wednesdays to Saturdays, but phone first to check.

**Getting There**
The church is within the Temple compound, just off Fleet Street. It is within easy walking distance of Underground stations at Temple, Blackfriars and Chancery Lane. It is also on numerous bus routes.

**Concessions**
Entry is free. Donations are voluntary.

**Facilities**

**INTERESTING FACT**
'The Round' shelters the effigies of nine knights including William Marshall, Earl of Pembroke, who helped persuade King John to sign the Magna Carta.

# Glasgow Cathedral

Glasgow Cathedral is one of the few Scottish churches to have survived the Reformation. Its origins date back to AD 550 when St Mungo, also known as St Kentigern – the patron saint and founder of the city of Glasgow – established a religious community known as Clas-Gu or 'dear family'. King Riderch of Strathclyde invited Mungo to become Archbishop of Strathclyde in AD 585.

St Mungo was buried close to the church after his death in 614. His tomb lies in what is now the centre of the Lower Choir on what is believed to be the actual site of his grave.

The first stone church on the site was consecrated in the presence of King David I in 1136. It occupied an area now covered by the nave, with part of the earlier church surviving to one side. The earliest visible parts of the church are the walls of the nave, which date back to rebuilding works undertaken in the early 1200s. By the mid-1200s much of the rest of the building had materialized. In 1451 the pope declared that a pilgrimage to Glasgow Cathedral would be as meritorious as one to Rome and footfall increased. In the fifteenth century three towers were built, two of which were lost in the 1800s. The Blacader Aisle was built on the site of St Mungo's original church.

During the Reformation the determination to destroy churches was as strong in Glasgow as anywhere. So what is unusual is that the people of Glasgow took up arms to *protect* the cathedral. It is the only medieval cathedral in mainland Scotland to have survived. After this time the building was segregated allowing it to serve three separate congregations, a decision that was reversed in the nineteenth century. The cathedral continues to change and adapt and has some spectacular new stained-glass windows.

*opposite Glasgow Cathedral at night.*

**Glasgow Cathedral**
**Castle Street**
**Glasgow**
**G4 0QZ**

Tel 0141 552 6891
www.glasgowcathedral.org

**Opening**
Daily. Times vary, so please check the website for further details. Guides are available from May to September.

**Getting There**
The cathedral is situated just off Castle Street in the centre of Glasgow. It is close to the M8, junction 15. Trains run to Glasgow and many local buses go past the cathedral. It is a 25-minute walk from the train station to the cathedral.

**Concessions**
Free entry, donations welcomed.

**Facilities**

**SPECIAL FEATURE**
The chapel of St John the Evangelist contains part of what is believed to be the well used by St Mungo in the late 500s.

# Salisbury Cathedral

Before 1220, there had been a cathedral at Old Sarum, an ancient site some two miles north of the present city. But in that year, local politics led to a decision to move the bishop's seat to the nearby water meadows. These circumstances meant that, unusually, Salisbury Cathedral was built over a comparatively short period – thirty-eight years – and to a unified design in the early English Gothic style, which emphasised height and light. Only a few sections of the building were added later: the cloisters, chapterhouse, tower and spire.

Adding the spire was a huge risk, particularly since the cathedral's foundations were only four feet deep, because of its nearness to the river. Attempts had been made at other cathedrals, which had collapsed

**SPECIAL FEATURE**
The clock housed in the north aisle dates from no later than 1386. It has no face and chimes on the hour. It is the oldest working clock in the country, possibly in the world.

as a result. But, a generation after the rest of the cathedral was built, Salisbury was not only given a spire, but one which, at 404 feet from tip to ground, remains the tallest in Britain. Buttresses and bracing arches were added to take the extra weight, but the columns of the central crossing still bend inwards visibly under the strain. It is still possible to view part of the inside of the tower, with its original wooden scaffolding, but the highest section can only be reached from the outside.

The chapter house is octagonal, with beautiful fan-vaulting, a graceful central pillar and a medieval frieze, showing Old Testament scenes. It is also home to the best-preserved of four surviving copies of the Magna Carta, the cornerstone of the British legal system.

Around the inside of the cathedral are various medieval chapels and tombs, some strikingly opulent. Outside the cloisters surround the largest garth, or green space, in Britain. The cathedral close, which in the seventeenth century was a buzzing area full of taverns, is now another peaceful green.

The views of Salisbury Cathedral painted by John Constable in the 1820s, across fields which have changed little to this day, are among the best known rural scenes in British art.

*opposite A view across the green to Salisbury Cathedral.*

195

# Tintern Abbey

At the end of the eleventh century in France, there was a reaction against what were seen as declining standards of conduct and morality within the monasteries of the dominant Benedictine order. The Cistercian order arose as part of this reaction. The first Cistercian abbeys gave rise to 'daughter' establishments, disseminating the Cistercian principles of asceticism, poverty and seclusion. These in turn fostered 'grand-daughter' foundations and Tintern was one of these.

The abbey was founded by Walter fitz Richard of Clare, Lord of Chepstow, in 1131. It was the first house of 'white monks' — as the Cistercians were known, because of the rough pale wool they wore — in Wales and only the second in the British Isles. The Cistercians rejected previous monastic sources of wealth, such as tithes and rents, so the cultivation

**Tintern Abbey**
**Tintern**
**Monmouthshire, NP16 6SF**

**Tel 01443 336000**
**www.cadw.wales.gov.uk**

**Opening**
The Abbey is open daily throughout the year, with the exception of 24–26 December and New Years Day.

**Getting There**
Trains between Cardiff and Gloucester call at Chepstow. Buses run from Chepstow and Monmouth to Tintern.

**Concessions**
Children under 15 years
Discabled and carers, Families

**Facilities**

of land became vitally important. To this end an extra labour supply was provided by lay brothers.

Initially, the monks would have lived in wooden buildings. But by the mid-twelfth century they had built a stone church and cloisters. The Gothic church that dominates the site was consecrated in 1301.Greatest among the abbey's benefactors was Roger Bigod, Earl of Norfolk, one of the most powerful figures in Edward I's court. As Lord of Chepstow, Bigod gave Tintern huge gifts of land, including a manor in Norfolk that

became the abbey's single most valuable asset. Bigod's generosity led many to see him as the abbey's founder.

Tintern prospered right up to the Dissolution, even through the period of the Black Death in 1349. But in 1536 it was surrendered to the king. The abbey was dismantled and ignored, before being rediscovered by the Romantic artists and poets of the eighteenth century. Excited by the ruins and their unique setting, their interest led to Tintern's preservation.

**SPECIAL FEATURE**
The west front of the abbey was completed shortly after 1300 and is typical of the architecture of the time: the huge window is a perfect example of the Decorated style.

*above Tintern Abbey.*

# Durham Cathedral

Durham Cathedral is a masterpiece of Norman architecture, an icon of the north and a World Heritage Site. It is the only English cathedral to retain almost all of its Norman craftsmanship and one of the few to preserve the integrity of the original design.

The cathedral was built to house the shrine of St Cuthbert. Cuthbert spent much of his life at Lindisfarne (see pages 186–187), but after his death in 687 and under the threat of a Viking invasion, the monks carried his body on their wanderings until they settled in Durham in 995. They also carried books with them so the cathedral library has its origins in the Lindisfarne monastery. Building work began in 1093 and was completed just forty years later. The cathedral towers over a precipitous gorge and is visible for miles around.

**Durham Cathedral
Durham
DH1 3EH**

**Tel 0191 3864266
www.durhamcathedral.co.uk**

**Opening**
The cathedral is open daily to sightseers, but may be closed for special services. Please check the website for further information

**Getting There**
Durham Cathedral is in the centre of the town. It is a 20-minute walk from the railway station or you can get the cathedral bus that runs every 20 minutes. Drivers should come off the A1 at junction 62.

**Concessions**
Free entry, donations welcomed.

**Facilities**

**INTERESTING FACT**
St Oswald, king of the Northumbrians, was known for his piety, generosity and alms-giving. Tradition holds that his head is buried inside St Cuthbert's tomb.

The Venerable Bede, whose body was moved to Durham around 1020, wrote the first history of the English people and lived from 673 to 735. He was reputed to be the greatest scholar of his time. According to legend the title 'Venerable' was given to him by an angel who filled in the inscription on his tomb.

The nave, choir and transepts are all Norman, but the western towers date from the twelfth and thirteenth centuries. The great central tower is the most recent addition; it has gothic detailing and was built in the fifteenth century. The original thirteenth century sanctuary knocker can be seen among the treasures of St Cuthbert: a replica hangs on the north porch door. The cloister, which was begun at the same time as the rest of the cathedral, contains much work from the fifteenth century.

The Reformation was a traumatic time in the cathedral's history. The monastery was surrendered to the crown in December 1540 and many historic furnishings and artefacts were destroyed. Things became even worse during the Civil War and the Commonwealth period. The cathedral was closed and used by Cromwell to incarcerate 3000 Scottish prisoners. With the Restoration a new Bishop, John Cosin, set about refurbishing the church and there is much ornate woodwork from this period.

*opposite Durham Cathedral on the River Wear.*

# Dunfermline Abbey

Dunfermline Abbey has played a central part in Scottish history. The cathedral was built by King David in memory of his mother Margaret, who fled to Dunfermline and the court of Malcolm I in 1066 with the royal party, following its defeat at the Battle of Hastings. Margaret was the daughter of Edward Atherling, a claimant to the English throne, and she married Malcolm in 1070.

The Celtic community built the first Christian church at Dunfermline in 800, but the foundation of the Abbey dates to the 1070s when Margaret founded a Benedictine priory, a project her son continued. It is the burial place of eight Scottish kings, four queens, five princes and two princesses. David I is interred here along with the legendary Robert the Bruce, allegedly buried without his heart.

The side walls of the central area of the medieval nave are carded on five massive pillars on the left and six on the right. Two pillars feature a chevron design that gives the illusion that they are unequal in diameter. Recessed into the floor are brass lines indicating the outline of the priory church of Queen Margaret and the Culdee (Celtic) church of the tenth century.

The church has a number of impressive stained-glass windows including the Malcolm and the Queen Margaret windows in the south transept.

The abbey was attacked and partially destroyed several times, but the nave was not touched. The more modern 'Place of Worship' was built in 1818 after the collapse of the monks' tower.

*below The Abbey and Palace from Pittencrief Park.*

**Dunfermline Abbey**
**St Margaret Street**
**Dunfermline**
**Fife**
**KY12 7PE**

**Tel 01383 724586**
**www.dunfermlineabbey.co.uk**

**Opening**
The abbey is open Monday – Saturdays from March – October. Sunday opening is limited, please see the website for more information.

**Getting There**
Dunfermline Abbey is situated high on a ridge in the middle of the town. There are regular trains from Edinburgh to Dunfermline, and the abbey is a 15-minute walk from the station.

**Concessions**
Entry is free, donations are welcome

**Facilities**

**INTERESTING FACT**
When in 1818 a new pulpit was installed over the tomb and memorial of Robert the Bruce, the king's remains were examined and measured before being re-interred.

# Coventry Cathedral

Coventry's earliest cathedral was founded as a Benedictine community by Leofric the Earl of Mercia in 1043, but with the Dissolution of the Monasteries in 1539 the see of Coventry and Lichfield was transferred to Lichfield, and the former cathedral fell into decay. In 1918 the modern diocese of Coventry was created and the church of St Michael designated as its cathedral.

On the night of 14 November 1940 the city of Coventry was devastated by bombs dropped by the Luftwaffe. The cathedral was hit by a number of incendiary devices and burned along with the city. The decision to rebuild the cathedral was taken the morning after its destruction, not in defiance, but as a sign of faith, trust and hope for the future of the world.

The cathedral stonemason noticed that two of the charred medieval roof timbers had fallen in the shape of a cross. He set them up in the ruins where they were later placed on an altar of rubble along with the words 'Father Forgive'.

The competition to redesign the cathedral was won by Basil Spence. The foundation stone was laid by the Queen in 1956 and the new cathedral was consecrated in 1962. The ruins remain hallowed ground and the two together create one living cathedral.

The cathedral is filled with the work of the leading artists of the time; Graham Sutherland's tapestry of Christ in Glory dominates the east end of the cathedral, while John Huttons' screen of saints and angels allows the spirit of the ruins to pervade the new cathedral. Coloured light streams through John Piper's Baptistry window and Epstein's St Michael and the Devil guards the cathedral steps.

*opposite The new Coventry Cathedral and the old Cathedral ruins.*

**Coventry Cathedral**
**Coventry, CV1 5AB**

**Tel 024 7652 1200**
**www.coventrycathedral.org.uk**

**Opening**
Open daily services permitting.

**Getting There**
Trains and coaches run to Coventry.

**Concessions**
Free entry, donations welcomed.

**Facilities**

**INTERESTING FACT**
A cross fashioned by three medieval nails found in the ruins by a local priest, has become a symbol of Coventry's international ministry of reconciliation.

# Stonehenge

The circles of mighty stones at Stonehenge form one of the most recognisable monuments in the world. It is also one of the most enigmatic.

It was not constructed as a coherent whole, but is the result of milennia of repositioning and re-use of the stones, all achieved with the most basic of tools.

The first stage of construction took place in around 3100 BC. It was a large circular bank-and-ditch ('henge') arrangement. Around the edge of the ditch were fifty-six 'Aubrey holes', about one metre wide and deep, the purpose of which is unclear. Shortly after this stage of development, the site was abandoned for more than 1000 years.

The second stage of building was dramatic. From around 2150 BC, some eighty-two bluestones, weighing up to four tonnes each, were moved from the Preseli mountains in Wales, 240 miles away. It is now thought they were transported mainly by water on rafts up a series of rivers. For the overland legs of the journey, the stones were moved on sledges and rollers. Once on site, they were levered into position in an incomplete double circle. At the same time, the orginal entrance was widened and part of the avenue was built, aligned with the sunrise at the summer solstice.

The third stage of construction, around 2000 BC, was, if anything, even more astonishing. The immense Sarsen stones, some weighing fifty tonnes, were brought from the Marlborough Downs near Avebury, twenty-five miles to the north. They were too heavy to float on water and must have been moved with sledges and ropes. It has been shown that it would need 500 men to pull each stone, with a further 100 to keep laying the rollers in front of the sledge. The Sarsens were laid in an outer circle. On top of them was placed a continuous run of lintels, secured by mortice and tenon joints derived from woodworking formation. In the centre, five vast trilithon stones were erected in a horseshoe.

Shortly after 1500 BC the bluestones were re-arranged in the horseshoe and circle arrangement seen today.

Stonehenge
Wiltshire
SP4 7DE

**Tel 01722 343834**
**www.english-heritage.org.uk/stonehenge**

**Opening**
Stonehenge is open daily, except 24–25 December.

**Getting There**
Stonehenge is 2 miles west of Amesbury on the A303. Trains call at Salisbury, 9 miles away. Buses run from Salisbury.

**Concessions**
Children 5–15 years; under 5s free
Families
Groups
National Trust members (free)
Over 60s
Students
Unemployed

**Facilities**

**INTERESTING FACT**
It is not known if Stonehenge's orientation to the rising and setting sun is because it was built by sun-worshippers, or because it was part of a giant astronomical calendar.

*opposite and overleaf Views of the ancient stones at Stonehenge.*

# Battle Abbey

1066 is probably the best-known date in English history. On 14 October of that year, William of Normandy defeated Harold of England and a new period of English history – and architecture – began. The battle actually took place some seven miles north of Hastings, at a place then called Senlac. The advantages and disadvantages of this location to both sides, have been much discussed, but it is possible that it was simply the only piece of open ground in a heavily forested area large enough for a battle. The Normans made good use of the strategy of false retreats, luring the Saxons into breaking ranks in pursuit, then cutting them down. This weakened the vital Saxon shield wall (initially some six to ten men thick) and eventually the Normans were able to break through. King Harold was killed, possibly by an arrow in the eye, although some scholars now believe he was cut down by an axe.

Battle Abbey was founded by William to commemorate his victory and possibly also as an act of penance for Harold's death and subsequent butchery on the field. Work on the abbey was started in 1070, after William had been crowned at Westminster Abbey and had asserted his authority over England by ruthlessly putting down several rebellions. Building started with the abbey church. The east front was completed within the year, but the west front was not finished until 1094, by which time William was dead, although his son William Rufus was present at the consecration. Almost nothing is left of the church today, except the outline of the apse and a stone marking the site of the high altar. This is reckoned to be the spot on which King Harold fell.

**SPECIAL FEATURE**
The Great Gatehouse was built in 1338 during the Hundred Years' War. It is widely regarded as the finest surviving monastic entrance in Britain.

**Battle Abbey**
**Battle**
**East Sussex, TN33 0AD**

**Tel 01424 773792**
**www.english-heritage.org.uk**
**/battleabbeyandbattlefield**

**Opening**
The brand new museum, and abbey and battlefield are open daily, except 24–26 December and New Years Day.

**Getting There**
In Battle town centre at the south end of the High Street. Battle train station is 0.5 mile away. Buses go to Battle from Maidstone and Hastings.

**Concessions**
Children 5–16 years; under 5s free
Families
Groups
Over 60s
Students
Unemployed

**Facilities**

Some later monastic buildings survive, including the dormitory range, which has a fine vaulted novices' chamber. But of the remodelling which took place in the late twelfth century, much was destroyed when the monastery was dissolved under Henry VIII. After the Dissolution, sections of the abbey became private homes; a school was also founded.

*opposite* The Great Gatehouse at Battle Abbey.

# York Minster

York Minster is the largest gothic cathedral north of the Alps, it was built between the twelfth and fifteenth centuries and has one of the finest collections of medieval stained glass in the world. It is world famous as an architectural masterpiece and is bursting with historical references.

York Minster dates back to 627 when Bishop Paulinus accompanied Ethelberga of Kent north for her wedding to Edwin of Northumbria. Edwin converted to Christianity and Bishop Paulinus baptised him in a rough wooden church, now regarded as the first York Minster. The church was rebuilt by St Wilfred around 670 and by Egbert (732–66), the first Archbishop of York, who created a fine cathedral school and library. York was thrown into turmoil over the next few centuries as Norse, Saxon, Danish and English invaders took the city. A Danish invasion completely destroyed the church in 1075 and the new Archbishop of York, Thomas of Bayeaux, started rebuilding the minster in 1080, only for it to be damaged again by fire in 1137.

Another reconstruction was started in 1220 with strong gothic influences. The central tower was built at the same time, but this collapsed in 1407. It was rebuilt and today you can climb 275 steps past medieval gargoyles up to the top to enjoy the view. The Norman nave was rebuilt around 1280 to twice its original dimensions, making it the widest in Europe. Work continued on the cathedral until 1472. York Minster has 128 windows in total, the most famous of which are the Five Sisters in the North Transept. The Chapter House is a masterpiece of medieval architecture with a ribbed wooden roof and traceried stained-glass windows.

York Minster
Deangate
York, YO1 7HH

Tel 01904 557216
www.yorkminster.org

**Opening**
Sightseeing daily from Monday to Saturday and Sunday afternoons. Closed Good Friday, Easter Sunday, Christmas Eve and Christmas Day. Special services or events may close the cathedral at short notice, so please check the website before visiting.

**Getting There**
York is just off the A64. Trains and coaches run from major cities in the UK to York. York Minster is a few minutes walk from the city centre.

**Concessions**
Children under 17 free
Over 60s, Students

**Facilities**

York Minster suffered terribly during and after the Reformation. Under Elizabeth I the interior of the minster was stripped bare even of its tombs. From there on the minster was prey to changing fashions; Lord Burlington laid a neo-classical floor, which required the destruction of every tomb left in the nave. Further fires during the Victorian period have necessitated a protracted programme of restoration works to preserve this extraordinary building.

*opposite York Minster.*

> **SPECIAL FEATURE**
> The central tower weighs 16,000 tonnes, the equivalent of forty Jumbo Jets. It is the tallest lantern tower in England at 198 feet high.

# Best of the Rest

# Hadrian's Wall

**Hadrian's Wall is one of the world's best known heritage attractions and is a World Heritage Site. Built to separate the Romans from the 'Barbarians' of the north, it formed the frontier of the Roman Empire in Britain for 300 years.**

The invasion of Britain took place in AD 43, under the Emperor Claudius, but in AD 70 Emperor Vespasian, having thus far penetrated only as far as the North of England, determined to conquer the whole island. Armies advanced northwards, but despite initial success were forced to withdraw. Claudius' successor, Hadrian (AD 117–AD 138), wanted to establish proper frontiers and – where no natural barrier, such as a river, existed – he built an artificial one.

The wall was built of stone for the eastern forty-eight miles and of stacked turf westwards to Solway. At one mile intervals there were fortlets, known as milecastles, attached to the rear of the wall with gateways through their north and south side. Between the milecastles, built approximately a third of a mile apart, were towers or turrets used for observation and signalling. A deep V-shaped ditch in front of the wall provided protection from the north, while to the south of the wall, a deep, flat-bottomed ditch, a *vallum*, prevented unauthorised access from within the province, except at controlled crossings. Settlements sprang up close to the forts attracted by the high pay of the soldiers.

It took Hadrian's army just four years to build the seventy-three mile barrier (eighty-four Roman miles) across the north of England, using one million cubic metres of stone. It was completed by AD 126. The wall stood fifteen feet high and was ten feet thick. Ten thousand auxiliary troops manned watchtowers and forts. Auxiliary units were raised in provinces newly absorbed by the Romans, but sent to other parts of the empire.

A network of forts, such as Segedunum, Chesters and Housestead, run along the length of the wall. These and the nine museums also dotted along its length display artefacts such as coins, pottery, armour, tools and writing tablets, which enable visitors to uncover the realities of Roman frontier life.

*opposite Aerial view of Hadrian's Wall showing the Vallum defensive ditch.*
*overleaf Near Housteads on Hadrian's Wall.*

**Hadrian's Wall runs through three counties: Tyne & Wear, Northumberland and Cumbria.**

**Tel 01434 322002**
**www.hadrians-wall.org**

**Opening**
Open throughout the year, some sites charge admission and opening times vary; please check the website for further information.

**Getting There**
The wall runs from Ravenglass on the west coast to South Tyneside on the east coast. Trains run to Newcastle. The AD122 bus runs the entire length of the wall and stops at Newcastle Central Station throughout the summer tourist season. Hadrian's cycleway allows cyclists to travel the length of the wall. The Hadrian's Wall Path National Trail is eighty-four miles long and allows walkers to traverse its length.

**Concessions**
Free entry to the public sections of Hadrian's Wall. Individual sites have entry fees; please check the website for further information.

**Facilities**
Facilities vary at sites along the wall.

## INTERESTING FACT

Two years into the construction of Hadrian's Wall it was decided to build sixteen forts along its length, to accommodate 500–1000 troops each.

# Sherwood Forest

Sherwood Forest is one of the most ancient areas of woodland left in Britain; flint tools used by prehistoric hunter-gatherers have been found, and there is evidence of Iron Age and Roman habitation. Nearly 500 acres have been preserved to reveal the true beauty of the ancient woodlands.

The first recorded use of the name Sherwood dates from AD 958 when the forest was called Sciryuda, meaning 'the woodland belonging to the shire'. After the Norman invasion of 1066 it became a royal hunting forest and was especially popular with both King John and Edward I. The ruins of King John's Hunting Lodge can be seen at Clipstone. The word 'forest' was a legally binding term meaning that the area and the timber and game within it were subject to royal jurisdiction.

Around the 1200s, the time of the legendary Robin Hood, Sherwood covered roughly 100,000 acres, or a fifth of the county of Nottinghamshire. It comprised oak and birch woodland interspersed with areas of grassland, sandy heath and three royal deer parks. Sherwood Forest was a productive, managed resource used to produce poles and laths for building, while twigs and brushwood were sold for fuel. The main London-to-York road ran straight through the forest leaving travellers at the mercy of outlaws. Nonetheless, cattle, sheep and deer grazed on the woodland pasture and pigs hunted for acorns in winter.

In the twelfth and thirteenth centuries Christian monks established large communities on lands given to them by the crown, but after the Dissolution much of the monastic land was sold into private ownership. Within the heart of the forest, however, the peasants continued to live as they always had.

Charles I was the last king to use Sherwood as a royal hunting forest. By the eighteenth century large swathes of land in Sherwood had been sold or gifted to noblemen. The industrialisation of the nineteenth and twentieth centuries imposed severe strain on Sherwood. Areas of the forest were requisitioned for military camps in World War II. Today Sherwood Forest

**Sherwood Forest National Nature Reserve**
**Edwinstowe**
**Nottinghamshire**
**NG21 9HN**

Tel 0845 330 4214
www.nottinghamshire.gov.uk/countryparks

**Opening**
Open daily except for Christmas Day.

**Getting There**
Sherwood Forest National Nature Reserve lies north of Edwinstowe, 2 miles from Ollerton and 15 miles north of Nottingham on the B6034. The nearest mainline railway station is Nottingham and trains run on to Mansfield and Newark, which are closer to the forest. Local buses run from Mansfield, Nottingham and Worksop.

**Concessions**
Free entry.

**Facilities**

### SPECIAL FEATURE
The Major Oak is at least 800 years old and weighs an estimated 83 tonnes. Its trunk circumference is 23 foot and its branches span more than 92 feet.

National Nature Reserve is a heritage site of international significance.

*opposite The Major Oak in Sherwood Forest.*

# Alton Towers

There is more to Alton Towers than the mighty theme park; the 500 acres of lavishly landscaped gardens are a visual delight. The fifteenth earl created them to be as different as possible in character and style to almost any other garden in England.

Alton Towers dates back to the eighth century when a fortress, held by Ceolred, king of Mercia, occupied the site. The earls of Shrewsbury took residence in 1412 and the estate remained with the family until 1924.

It was the fifteenth earl, Charles Talbot, born in 1753, who tamed the landscape with the help of hundreds of artisans, mechanics and labourers. The two principal garden architects were Robert Abrahams (1774–1850) and Thomas Allason (1790–1852), whose combined architectural talent and eye for beauty, allied to the earl's deep pockets, made the gardens so grandiose.

Under the direction of the earl, Abrahams designed and built the Chinese Pagoda Fountain as an exact copy of the To Ho Pagoda in Canton. To supply this fountain with water, he had to dig out lakes, pools and terraces to encourage the flow of water from a spring at Ramshorn into the lower extremity of the valley gardens. This fountain had the capacity to throw a volume of water ninety feet above the tree tops, where it now seemingly teases the Skyride cable car that crosses the valley gardens.

The Bath Fountain was constructed under the direction of John Talbot. This beautiful small pond with a figure of Triton blowing water through a conch shell was renovated in the summer of 1994. The Grand Conservatories, designed and built by Abrahams, are a breathtaking structure stretching 300 feet in length and made of galvanised iron and plate glass.

Charles Talbot was a man who enjoyed spending lavishly on shows and entertainment. He housed a blind Welsh harpist in a quaint thatched cottage, known as Swiss Cottage; the harpist was employed to fill the garden with music for the delight of the earl and his family. A cenotaph to Charles Talbot stands near the garden entrance bearing the inscription 'He Made the Desert Smile'.

**Alton Towers**
**Alton**
**Staffordshire**
**ST10 4DB**

Tel 08705 204060
www.altontowers.com

**Opening**
Open daily from March to November. For further details please check the website.

**Getting There**
Alton Towers is in the heart of Staffordshire and is accessible from the M1 and M6. The nearest railway station is Stoke-on-Trent and packages including bus transfers are available. A number of buses run to Alton Towers; please check the website for further information.

**Concessions**
The gardens are accessed via the Theme Park – there is no separate ticket. Children 4–12 years; under 4s free Families, Over 60s

**Facilities**

**INTERESTING FACT**
The gardens were first opened to the public in 1860 when fêtes drawing crowds of 30,000 were common. Entertainers included lion tamers, elephants and bands.

*opposite The Chinese Pagoda in the gardens at Alton Towers.*

# The Cabinet War Rooms
# and Churchill Museum

The Cabinet War Rooms were created in 1938 as a response to the threat of Hitler's ever-increasing power in Germany. They were situated in what was then the basement of the Office of Public Works.

On inspecting the Cabinet Room in 1940, Churchill announced: 'This is the room from which I will direct the war'. It duly became the centre of operations not only for the war cabinet, comprising members from all sides in parliament, but also for the Defence Committee of the Chiefs of Staff.

Churchill was given to holding meetings late into the night. This, along with the threat of air raids on London which often made 10 Downing Street unsafe, led to the creation of a bedroom for the Prime Minister, which also functioned as a study and meeting room. It was not unknown for Churchill to start the day giving dictation from his bed, while smoking a cigar. It was also from this room that Churchill made four international broadcasts in the bleak second half of 1940, when most of central Europe had fallen to the Nazis. A communicating door leads to the Map Room, where large charts of the theatres of war can still be seen on the walls.

The Cabinet War Rooms were expanded throughout the early 1940s. One improvement was the conversion of a broom cupboard into a transatlantic telephone room. Here Churchill could speak directly to President Roosevelt, via an improved telephone scrambler. This machine was known as 'Sigsaly'; its London terminal was so vast it was housed in the basement of Selfridges department store. Partially-encrypted messages were sent there from the War Rooms, and then on to Washington by radio.

The Cabinet Rooms were closed at the end of the war in 1945, and left untouched. In 1948, parliament declared them a Site of National Significance, which ensured their preservation.

*opposite The Map Room in the Cabinet War Rooms.*

## SPECIAL FEATURE

The Churchill Museum was opened in 2005. It is the first dedicated to his life and contains large numbers of mementos, interactive displays and timelines.

**Cabinet War Rooms
King Charles Street
London
SW1A 2AQ**

**Tel 020 7930 6961
www.iwm.org.uk**

**Opening**
Open daily, except 24–26 December.

**Getting There**
Westminster and St. James's Park are the nearest Underground stations. Numerous local buses. Ferry services to Westminster Pier.

**Concessions**
Children under 16 free
Disabled (carers free)
Over 60s
Pre-booked groups (10 or more)
Students

**Facilities**

# Clifton Suspension Bridge

**Isambard Kingdom Brunel's famous Clifton Suspension Bridge spans the Avon gorge and is a symbol of the city of Bristol.**

In 1754 a Bristol wine merchant left a legacy to build a bridge over the gorge. A design competition was held in 1829 and judged by Thomas Telford. Declaring that all the designs were unsuitable he submitted his own, but the decision to declare him the winner was unpopular.

A second competition was held in 1830 and twenty-four-year-old Isambard Kingdom Brunel's design was declared the best. It was his first major commission and he was appointed project engineer.

The foundation stone was laid in 1831, but work was beset by political and financial difficulties and the project was abandoned in 1843 with only the towers completed.

When work recommenced six wire ropes were taken across the gorge, secured and tightened. These were planked and bound with iron hoops to make a footpath and wire handrails were added. People could pay to be pulled across the gorge in a basket, and it was fashionable to propose to your loved one on the way over. Two men died during its construction.

Pilots used to fly under the bridge in the 1930s, but the last fixed-wing flight was in 1957 when, in spite of a ban, Flying Officer Crossley flew a Vampire

**Clifton Suspension Bridge**
**Bridge Road**
**Leigh Woods**
**Bristol**
**BS8 3PA**

**Tel 0117 9744664**
**www.clifton-suspension-bridge.org.uk**

**Opening**
The bridge is very occasionally closed for events; please check the web site for further information.

**Getting There**
Clifton Suspension Bridge is two miles west of Bristol's city centre. Trains run from London Paddington to Bristol Temple Meads. Buses 8, 8A, 9 and 9A run to Clifton Village or Christ Church Clifton and the bridge is a short level walk from these bus stops.

**Concessions**
It costs 50 pence to cross the bridge by car, and is free by bicycle or on foot.

**Facilities**

jet underneath the bridge at 450 miles per hour. He crashed into the cliffs and was killed instantly.

Brunel died prematurely at the age of fifty-three. The bridge was completed as his memorial and finally opened in 1864 – thirty-four years after he was declared winner of the design competition. It cost £100,000 to build.

It is a spectacular piece of design standing 245 feet above high water; the suspension chains are still the originals and are regularly checked, it is estimated that they will last for centuries more. Although the Clifton Suspension Bridge was designed for light horse-drawn vehicles it meets modern demands and today some 12,000 motor vehicles cross it daily.

**INTERESTING FACT**

In 1885 Sarah Anne Henley threw herself from the bridge after an argument with her boyfriend. Her crinoline petticoats slowed her fall and, despite injury she lived to 84!

*below Brunel's Clifton Suspension Bridge.*

# Portmeirion

The extraordinary village of Portmeirion is set on its own private peninsula on the southern shores of Snowdonia. It was developed by Welsh architect Clough Williams-Ellis to prove that a naturally beautiful site could be developed without spoiling it. It is world famous for its beauty and as the location of the cult television series *The Prisoner*.

Bertram Clough Williams-Ellis acquired the site for Portmeirion in 1925 for less than £5000. It was an abandoned, neglected wilderness on a beautiful promontory, and was then called Aber Iâ (Glacial Estuary). Clough changed its name to Port, indicating its seaside location and Merion from the county in which it then sat – Merioneth. The first article about

**Portmeirion**
**Gwynedd**
**LL48 6ET**

**Tel 01766 770000**
**www.portmeirion-village.com**

**Opening**
Open daily, except Christmas Day.

**Getting There**
Portmeirion is 1.5 miles south of Porthmadog. The nearest mainline train station is Bangor and a taxi ride from Bangor to Portmeirion takes 45 minutes. There are Cambrian Coast and Ffestiniog railway stations in the village of Minffordd about a mile away.

**Concessions**
Children 5–16 years; under 5s free
Families
Over 60s, Students

**Facilities**

it appeared in *The Architect's Journal* in 1926 with a photograph of a scale model. Clough wanted to explore the concept that although houses are designed with care, towns may grow by chance.

The village was built in two stages, the first from 1925–39 when it was pegged out and the most distinctive buildings were constructed in an Arts and Crafts style. In the second stage of building work, between 1954–76, Clough filled in the details in a classical or Palladian style. Several buildings were salvaged from demolition sites, which caused Clough to nominate Portmeirion as 'a home for fallen buildings'.

Clough's motto was, 'Cherish the past, adorn the present and construct for the future'. The village consists of around fifty buildings, most of which are self catering houses for holiday accommodation or hotels. All have a fascinating history. The climate at Portmeirion is mild and temperate, so exotic and tender plant species thrive here.

Portmerion is world famous as the location for the enigmatic cult television series *The Prisoner*, starring Patrick McGoohan, which was filmed between 1966 and 1976. McGoohan, Number 6, uttered the now infamous line, 'I am not a number, I am a free man'.

**INTERESTING FACT**
In 1951 a fire devastated Clough's home, Plas Brondanw. Clough's false teeth, spectacles and the family silver were all ruined.

*above The distinctive Portmeirion Village.*

# Bletchley Park

**Bletchley Park is the historic site of code-breaking activities during World War II and the birthplace of the modern computer.**

It was built by Sir Herbert Leon who bought the land in 1883 and turned it into his country estate. Under threat of demolition in 1939, the government intervened; with the threat of war looming the Government Code and Cipher School, based in London, needed a safer home where it could work undisturbed by air raids.

Bletchley Park was given the cover name Station X, being the tenth of a number of sites MI6 acquired for wartime operations. The code breakers arrived in August 1939, masquerading as 'Captain Ridley's shooting party' to disguise their identity.

The Enigma machine was the backbone of German military intelligence and its complex and bewildering code was thought to be unbreakable. Keys were attached to electrical circuits, and the raw material came from wireless intercept stations dotted around Britain.

With the declaration of peace all code-breaking activity ceased and the thousands who worked there departed. It was not until wartime data were declassified in the 1970s that the true story emerged and in 1991, as it was about to be sold, it was decided to preserve the site for posterity. Bletchley Park today reveals its fascinating code-breaking history and allows visitors to see a slice of wartime life.

*below Bletchley Park.*

**The Mansion
Bletchley Park
Milton Keynes
MK3 6EB**

**Tel 01908 640404
www.bletchleypark.org.uk**

**Opening**
Open daily except 25–26 December and New Year's Day.

**Getting There**
Bletchley Park is 50 miles north-west of London and close to Milton Keynes, just off Junction 14 of the M1. Trains run to Milton Keynes and to Bletchley. The railway station is a short walk. Buses run to Bletchley from Milton Keynes.

**Concessions**
Children 12–16 years; under 12s free
Families
Over 60s
Students

**Facilities**

**INTERESTING FACT**
The rotors and wires of the Enigma machine had numerous configurations. The odds against being able to break the code were 150 million million million to one.

# Sutton Hoo

In AD 410 the Roman emperor Honorius withdrew his army from Britain. As Roman influence declined, people from Denmark, Germany and the Lower Rhine gradually arrived. These newcomers displaced or enslaved the previous Celtic inhabitants. The settlers became known as Anglo-Saxons. Their languages merged into Old English and became the basis for our modern speech. They also formed kingdoms, each with its own ruler, laying the foundations for present-day England.

Although Christianity was beginning to arrive from Ireland and France, the Anglo-Saxons were predominantly pagan. Important rulers were often buried in ceremonial mounds, with precious goods as a sign of their status. The burials at Sutton Hoo shed light on a little understood period of our history, when Britain hovered between the old religions and the new.

In 1938, Mrs Edith Pretty, who owned the land, asked a local archaeologist, Basil Brown, to examine some ancient burial mounds near her house. Initially, they found only fragments. But in 1939 Brown made a trench in the largest mound and found iron ship rivets. Although ship burials were known in Scandinavia, they were very rare in Britain, and unique to East Anglia. This was an elaborate construction, in which a tomb had effectively been built into the keel. The wooden structure had rotted away, but the timbers had stained the sandy soil, leaving an outlined image.

Within the ship — which was ninety foot long —
were found beautifully crafted weapons, symbolic
objects and ornaments, some in gold and silver,
originating from Scandinavia, France and Byzantium.
Clearly, the grave belonged to someone of enormous
power, quite probably a local king.

Since the finds were made on the eve of World
War II, they were removed and taken to London where
they were safely stored in the Underground system.
More excavations took place in two phases between
the 1960s and the 1990s, investigating the whole
cemetery area. The ship treasures are held by the
British Museum, but there are also exhibitions at
the site.

*above Winter sunrise at Sutton Hoo.*

**SPECIAL FEATURE**
The iconic Sutton Hoo helmet has been
reconstructed from fragments. It is made of
iron with bronze decorative plates and is one
of only four known Anglo-Saxon helmets.

# Sir John Soane's Museum

**Sir John Soane's museum is packed with pieces selected and hoarded by the famous architect. The house was bequeathed to the nation by Soane and is still preserved much as he instructed.**

Sir John Soane, the son of a country bricklayer made good, is best known for designing the old and magnificent Bank of England building. He picked up many ideas for his work while on a grand tour of Italy. He married into money and built his own house at 13 Lincoln's Inn Fields, which is topped by an extraordinary glass dome that seems to light up the house. All in all Soane demolished and rebuilt three houses on the north side of Lincoln's Inn Fields. He was appointed Professor of Architecture at the Royal Academy in 1806 and began to collect books, models and casts so that students could visit and learn from them. He opened his house to students the day before and the day after he lectured. He negotiated an Act of Parliament in 1833 to settle and preserve the house and its collections for the benefit of students of architecture and amateur enthusiasts.

The house is thus preserved for posterity and little has changed since Soane died in 1837. Statuary and paintings are on show and include Turner, Canaletto, and Watteau. Over 20,000 architectural drawings can be seen, including some by Christopher Wren and Robert Adam and the original *Rake's Progress* by Hogarth is displayed in a special gallery.

The eclectic collection also includes Egyptian and classical antiquities, such as the Sarcophagus of Seti I and the only known surviving stone structures from the fourteenth century House of Lords. The Naseby Jewel is shown along with casts, stained glass, Chinese tiles, a collection of watches and clocks, and furniture including Horace Walpole's writing desk. In addition there is a miscellany of building materials: old nails, screws, window frames, and sash lifts from the early nineteenth century. The building and its contents seem to have been frozen in time, for which reason the evocative candlelight tours are highly recommended.

*opposite Sir John Soane's Museum in Lincoln's Inn Fields.*

**Sir John Soane's Museum
13 Lincoln's Inn Fields
London, WC2A 3BP**

**Tel 0207 405 2107
www.soane.org**

**Opening**
Open daily Tuesdays to Saturdays, closed Bank Holidays and Christmas Eve. Disabled access is limited; please check the website for further information. Candlelit evenings take place on the first Tuesday of every month.

**Getting There**
The museum is a short walk from Holborn Underground station.

**Concessions**
Free entry.

**Facilities**

**SPECIAL FEATURE**
The Naseby Jewel is a hat pin in the figure of a cavalier, studded with rubies, and said to have been dropped by Charles I at the Battle of Naseby in 1645.

# Brewery Arts Centre

The Brewery Arts Centre has moved from ale to art in the last 250 years. It was the first Brewery in the area, licensed in 1758. The business prospered and was taken over by William Mark – in 1858 a new brewery was built.

The boom time for the brewery was in the 1930s, when it supplied thirty pubs across Westmoreland with its famous Auld Kendal brew. It was decided to close the brewery in the late 1960s and the last brew was produced there in September 1968.

The Grade III listed building was purchased in 1970 by the Lake District Theatre Trust with a view to opening an Arts Centre. This opened in 1972 initially consisting of only a small theatre. It was refurbished in 1998.

A nod to the heritage of the Arts Centre remains; The Malt Room is the former racking room and cask store. The sugar store has become a photographic gallery and the Green Room restaurant was once the malt hopper.

*opposite Kendal's vibrant Arts Centre.*

**The Brewery Arts Centre**
**Highgate**
**Kendal**
**Cumbria**
**LA9 4HE**

**Tel 01539 725133**
**www.breweryarts.co.uk**

**Opening**
Open daily except Christmas Day.

**Getting There**
The Brewery Arts Centre is situated just off Junction 36 of the M6. The nearest train station is Oxenholme, which is 10 minutes away by taxi.

**Concessions**
Concessionary rates vary for different facilities.

**Facilities**

**SPECIAL FEATURE**
The Brewery Arts Centre is now a multi-purpose arts complex presenting a year-round programme of theatre, music, films, lectures and exhibitions.

# Oxford Colleges

Oxford University is the oldest seat of learning in the English-speaking world and has been an internationally renowned centre of scholarship and research for nine centuries. Matthew Arnold famously described Oxford thus: 'And that sweet city with her dreaming spires, she needs not June for beauty's heightening.'

The university does not have a definitive foundation date, but teaching has occurred there in some form since 1096. Initially a teaching centre for clerics, it developed rapidly after 1167 when Henry II forbade English students from attending the University of Paris. Most of the beautiful, pale gold colleges are clustered around the High Street and Broad Street. Balliol, University and Merton colleges are the oldest, being established between 1249 and 1264.

A walk around the Oxford colleges takes you in the footsteps of the great and the good. John Wycliffe, a fourteenth-century master at Balliol, campaigned here for a bible in English against the wishes of the pope. During the reformation, Anglican churchmen Cranmer, Latimer and Ridley were burnt for heresy outside Balliol in 1555. The deer in the park at Magdalen (pronounced 'maudlin') were originally brought in to make the aristocratic students from centuries past feel at home.

Christ Church, known as The House, was founded by Cardinal Wolsey and called Cardinal College, but Wolsey fell from favour, and it was later refounded as Christ Church in 1546. It is home to England's smallest cathedral; a Norman building with windows by Burne-Jones and William Morris, which serves as the college chapel. The famous Tom Tower is here, containing Great Tom: a seven-tonne bell designed by Sir Christopher Wren. Each evening at five past nine the bell rings 101 times to warn students that the gates are about to close. You can stroll through Christ Church Meadows to the river, a stretch of the Thames popularly known as the Isis.

Boar's Hill outside the city is the best place to see the perfect view of the spires. The university Church of St Mary the Virgin, first mentioned in the Domesday Book, also offers a stunning view from its tower.

*opposite The Cloisters at Magdalene College, Oxford.*

**Many colleges are scattered around Oxford's High Street and on Broad Street.**

**Tel 01865 270010 (University Information)**
**01865 726871 (Tourist Information)**
**www.ox.ac.uk**

**Opening**
Most colleges are open daily between 2pm and 5pm. However dates vary, please check college websites for further information.

**Getting There**
Oxford University is 57 miles north-west of London and is situated in the heart of the city. Trains run from Paddington to Oxford regularly and coaches run from London Victoria to Oxford. The colleges are a 15-minute walk from the station.

**Concessions**
The concessionary rates to visit individual colleges vary, so check individual college websites for further information.

**Facilities**
Facilities vary, so check individual college websites for further information.

**INTERESTING FACT**
In the thirteenth century rioting between students and town folk over indifferent wine served at the Swyndlestock Tavern, saw students killed and colleges ransacked.

# Charles Dickens Museum

The Charles Dickens Museum is housed in the only surviving London home of Dickens, one of the greatest British authors.

Dickens, also known by his pseudonym 'Boz', moved to 48 Doughty Streeth one year after his marriage and lived here for twenty-one months between April 1837 and December 1839. In a burst of amazing productivity in the short time he was at the house, he completed *The Pickwick Papers* and *Oliver Twist* and wrote *Nicholas Nickleby* in its entirety.

**Charles Dickens Museum**
**48 Doughty Street**
**London**
**WC1N 2LX**

**Tel 0207 405 2127**
**www.dickensmuseum.com**
**email: info@dickensmuseum.com**

**Opening**
Open daily except 25–26 December, but sometimes special events are organised over the festive season; please check the website. Disabled access is limited; please check the website for information.

**Getting There**
The Charles Dickens Museum is in central London: the nearest Underground stations are Russell Square, Holborn and Chancery Lane. The following buses go past the museum: 7, 17, 19, 38, 45, 46, 55, and 243.

**Concessions**
Children 5–16 years; under 5s free
Families
Over 60s
Students

**Facilities**

## INTERESTING FACT
Charles Dickens' family spent time in Marshalsea Debtors' prison while he, aged twelve, was sent to work in a factory. His father was the inspiration for Mr Micawber.

Dickens was only able to move his family here from his cramped rooms at Furnival's Inn in Holborn after the successful serialisation of *The Pickwick Papers*. Both ends of Doughty Street were sealed off at the time by gates manned by porters.

Two of Dickens' three children were born at Doughty Street. Tragically his sister-in-law, Mary Hogarth, suddenly became ill and died in his arms here, an incident he recalled when creating Little Nell's death scene in *The Old Curiosity Shop*. After his third child was born in October 1839 Dickens began looking for a larger house, which he could, by then, afford. The family moved to 1 Devonshire Terrace, Regents Park which was demolished in 1959. The Doughty Street house was under threat in 1923, but the Dickens Fellowship raised the mortgage and purchased the freehold; the museum was opened to the public in 1925.

The four-storey townhouse presents a window onto Dickensian London and is filled with memorabilia associated with this beloved author. It has the world's most important collection of Dickens artefacts; there are paintings by W.P. Frith and J.E. Millais, rare editions, letters, original manuscripts and furniture. There is even a grandfather clock that belonged to Moses Dickens, after whom Dickens named a character in *The Pickwick Papers*. Ongoing exhibitions reveal different slices of his life and the impact he had on Victorian society; after he wrote *Nicholas Nickleby* all the schools in Yorkshire were closed down!

*opposite Dickens' family home in Doughty Street.*

# SS Great Britain

The SS *Great Britain*, designed by Isambard Kingdom Brunel, was the world's first great ocean-going liner. She is one of the technological forerunners of modern shipping and symbolises the birth of international travel.

She was originally conceived as a paddle steamer, but builders quickly realised the advantages that the new technology of screw propulsion could confer, so they converted the ship and her engines to power a sixteen-foot propeller. At the time of her launch in 1843 she was the largest ship in the world, at least 100 foot longer than any of her rivals. She was the first ocean-going, screw-propelled, wrought-iron ship.

SS *Great Britain* carried 252 passengers and 130 crew and was designed for the luxury transatlantic-crossing trade. She ran aground on the sands of Dundrum Bay, Northern Ireland, in 1846, her engines were ruined and the expense of floating her forced her sale.

She acquired new owners, Gibbs Bright & Co, in 1852, who rebuilt her as a fast and luxurious emigrant carrier for travel to Australia. She was redesigned to carry 750 passengers in three classes. She averaged sixty days out and sixty days home and made thirty-two trips over the next twenty-four years carrying over 15,000 emigrants, many to the Australian Gold Rush.

By the late 1870s SS *Great Britain* was showing her age and could no longer be registered to carry passengers. Her engines were removed and she was converted into a sailing ship and used to carry Welsh coal to San Francisco via the notorious Cape Horn. On her third trip she ran into trouble and had to seek shelter in the Falkland Islands. She remained there throughout World War I replenishing battlecruisers with coal from her hold and thus played her part in

the battle of the Falkland Islands in December 1914. In 1937 she was no longer watertight and was towed out of Port Stanley harbour and sunk. Despite various attempts to rescue her she was not refloated until 1970, but is now fully restored as the world's first ocean-going liner and brilliantly reveals the realities of ocean travel.

*opposite SS Great Britain in Bristol Docks.*

**SS *Great Britain***
**Great Western Dockyard**
**Gas Ferry Road**
**Bristol**
**BS1 6TY**

**Tel 0117 929 1843**
**www.ssgreatbritain.org**

**Opening**
Open Daily except for 17, 24 and 25 December. For further dates please check website.

**Getting There**
Trains from London Paddington to Bristol Temple Meads. SS *Great Britain* is a 40-minute walk from the station, or take bus number 500. Ferries can be taken a few minutes walk from the train station.

**Concessions**
Children 5–15 years; under 5s free
Families
Over 60s, Students

**Facilities**

**INTERESTING FACT**
Between 1855 and 1856 the SS *Great Britain* was used as a troop ship during the Crimean War; she carried over 44,000 troops.

# The Roman Baths at Bath

The baths and temple complex at Bath – or *Aquae Sulis* as the Romans called the site – are centred around Britain's only hot spring. The strength and reliability of the spring enabled the Roman architects to construct an unusually large bath complex, including full-size hot swimming pools. Normally, heating the water for pools of that size would have been too costly. But with seven million litres a day emerging from the ground, at 46°C, they could afford to be ambitious.

The site had both a religious and a recreational function. There is evidence that some sort of worship

**The Roman Baths
Abbey Churchyard
Bath
BA1 1LZ**

**Tel 01225 477785
www.romanbaths.co.uk**

**Opening**
The baths are open daily throughout the year, including Bank Holidays, except 24–26 December and New Years Day. Further details are available from the website.

**Getting There**
The baths are in the city centre. Trains run to Bath Spa from London (Paddington and Waterloo) and several major cities, including Bristol, Southampton and Portsmouth.

**Concessions**
Children 6–16 years; under 5s free
Groups (10 or more)
Over 65s
Students
Unemployed

**Facilities**

> **SPECIAL FEATURE**
> The Pump Room was added in the eighteenth century, for socializing and drinking the supposedly healthy water. It was regarded as the heart of the city. It still is.

was taking place on the site before the arrival of the Romans. But they made it their own. The first temple had the spring in the corner of its open courtyard; later a vaulted roof was erected over it. This eventually collapsed into the spring in the sixth or seventh century BC, but the oak piles still provide a stable foundation for the extant buildings. In the first century AD, an impressive classical temple was built, one of only two in the country. By the second century AD, the temple was changed piecemeal into the more familiar Romano-Celtic form.

Worship continued at the site until the late fourth century when, with the advance of Christianity, the Emperor Theodosius ordered the closure of all pagan temples.

The Roman complex focuses on the Great, East and West baths. The West bath has some exceptionally well-preserved *stilae* – stone props around which hot air was circulated to heat the floor above them. The *Laconicum*, a round sauna or steam-room, is another unusual feature. The King's Bath was added in the twelfth century and was in use for therapeutic bathing until the middle of the twentieth century.

The Romans were skilled engineers. They built an extensive drainage system to return water from the baths to the river Avon and allow for maintenance to be carried out. Parts of it still contain the original wooden boards.

*opposite The Roman Baths with Bath Abbey in the background.*

# Cambridge Colleges

Cambridge is a compact city housing one of the oldest universities in the world. Walk in the footsteps of former illustrious students through the distinctive college buildings and green spaces.

The first Cambridge scholars arrived in 1209, seeking refuge from the angry townsfolk of Oxford. By 1226 numbers had risen sufficiently to establish a more formal organisation, represented by a chancellor and with an official course of study, but problems with

**Many colleges are scattered around the centre of the city, notably in King's Parade, Trinity Street and Trumpington Street. The 'Visit Cambridge' Visitor Information Centre is on Wheeler Street.**

**Tel 0871 226 8006 (Tourist Information)**
**www.cam.ac.uk**

**Opening**
Most colleges are open daily, but dates and opening times vary from college to college. Please check college websites for further information. Colleges are generally closed during the examination period in May and June.

**Getting There**
Cambridge is 50 miles north of London. Trains run regularly from London King's Cross and coaches run from Victoria Coach Station. Buses run to the city centre from the train station and bicycles can be hired near the train station. Punts can be found at the bottom of Silver Street.

**Concessions**
The concessionary rates to visit individual colleges vary, so check college websites for further information.

**Facilities**
Facilities vary so check individual college websites for further information.

the locals erupted again. Students were young and boisterous, often just fourteen or fifteen years of age and a disruptive influence in the city. The locals in turn aggravated relations by demanding exorbitant rents. Henry III resolved matters as early as 1231 by taking the scholars under his protection and sheltering them from landlord exploitation.

Peterhouse was the first college to be founded in 1284, by Hugo de Balsham, the Bishop of Ely. King's followed in 1317, its founder, Edward II, intending that it should supply recruits to the higher civil service. Ten more colleges were founded during the fifteenth and sixteenth centuries including Jesus College in 1496, with Thomas Cranmer as a former

pupil, and Christ's College in 1505, with Milton as a former student; his mulberry tree can still be seen in the grounds.

Henry VI raised funds to build King's College Chapel and determined that it should be without equal in size and beauty. No other college has a chapel built on such a grand scale. Work was interrupted by the Wars of the Roses, but was then resumed courtesy of the much-maligned Richard III. Henry VII and Henry VIII continued to fund the building, which took just over 100 years to complete.

A delightful way to see the college buildings and gardens is to punt along the River Cam, through The Backs (the rear of the colleges); float past Queens'

(founded 1448), King's, Clare (founded 1326), Trinity (founded 1546) and finally St John's (founded 1511), where you will come across the neo-gothic chapel, designed by George Gilbert Scott between 1863 and 1869 and known locally as the Wedding Cake.

*above* King's College Chapel, Cambridge.

### INTERESTING FACT
Cromwell attended Sidney Sussex College. Later construction of Clare College was delayed by the Civil War when he plundered the site for building stone.

# HMS *Victory*

HMS *Victory* – forever associated with Admiral Lord Nelson and the Battle of Trafalgar – is the oldest ship still in commission in the Royal Navy. She is also one of only two surviving ships of the line, the fore-runner of the modern battleship.

The decision to build *Victory* was taken in 1758. She was intended from the start to be a big ship, 227ft (69.34m) long and 205ft (62.5m) high, with 106 guns. This grand scale was unusual at a time when the trend was for smaller, more manoeuvrable vessels. Her designer was Sir Thomas Slade, at the time Surveyor of the Navy. The ship was named in 1760 after the preceding '*annus mirabilis*', or 'year of victories', when Britain had won several triumphs in the Seven Years War. *Victory* was launched in 1765, but lay unused for thirteen years, until France joined the American War of Independence against the British.

By 1798, HMS *Victory* was sufficiently damaged to be sent to Chatham for use as a hospital ship, but the loss of another important vessel led to her being reconditioned for active service.

Nelson first raised his flag on HMS *Victory* in 1803. But it was not until October 1805 that, with her as his flagship, he faced and defeated the combined French and Spanish fleet off Cape Trafalgar, losing his life in the process.

HMS *Victory* sailed in numerous further expeditions after Trafalgar, but was retired from frontline duty in 1812 when she was moored at Portsmouth. In 1889 she was converted to a naval school of telegraphy and served that purpose for some fifteen years. But as time passed she was allowed to rot, until in 1921 a campaign was started to save her and she was moved to the oldest dry dock in the world,

also at Portsmouth. In 1928, a plaque marking the completion of restoration was unveiled by George V.

HMS *Victory* is now both a museum and the flagship of the Commander-in-Chief, Naval Home Command.

*opposite HMS Victory, at dry dock in Portsmouth.*

**INTERESTING FACT**
HMS *Victory* acquired her distinctive yellow-and-black colouring in 1800. The 'Nelson chequer' was adopted by all Royal Navy ships after Trafalgar.

# Index

Page numbers in *italics* indicate illustrations.

# Picture Credits

168-169 © Geoffrey Morgan/Alamy
171 © Eric Nathan/Alamy
173 © Robert Harding Picture Library Ltd/Alamy
174-175 © NTPL/Oliver Benn
177 © Simon Wilkinson/Alamy
178 © Topix/Alamy
181 © David Lyons/Alamy
183 © BL Images Ltd/Alamy
184-185 © English Heritage Photo Library
186 © Michael Jenner/Alamy
189 © Bildarchiv Monhelm GmbH/Alamy
190 © PjrFoto.com/Phil Robertson/Alamy
193 © David Robertson/Alamy
194 © James Hughes/Alamy
196-197 © M Ritrich/Alamy
199 © BL Images Ltd/Alamy
200-201 © David Robertson/Alamy
203 © John Martin/Alamy
204 © English Heritage Photo Library
206-207 © English Heritage Photo Library
208 © English Heritage Photo Library
211 © Jon Arnold Images/Alamy
212-213 © David Entrican/Alamy
215 © Skyscan Photolibrary/Alamy
216-217 © David Robertson/Alamy

218 © Robert Estall photo agency/Alamy
220 © Sally A Morgan; Ecoscene/Corbis
222 © POPPERFOTO/Alamy
224-225 © Gavin Newman/Alamy
226-227 © nagelestock.com/Alamy
228-229 © Ian Miles – Flashpoint Pictures/Alamy
230-231 © NTPL/Joe Cornish
233 © Neil Setchfield/Alamy
234-235 © David Crausby/Alamy
236 © nagelestock.com/Alamy
239 © Justin Kase/Alamy
240 © Liquid Light/Alamy
243 © Hideo Kurlhara/Alamy
244-245 © Travel Ink/Alamy
247 © Adrian Chinery/Alamy

Front cover © Rolf Richardson/Alamy
Back cover (clockwise from top left) © Jon Arnold
Images/Alamy, © POPPERFOTO/Alamy, © AA World
Travel Library/Alamy, © NTPL/Andrew Butler

We apologise in advance for any unintentional
omission or neglect and will be pleased to insert
the appropriate acknowledgement for any companies
or individuals in any subsequent edition of this work.

# Acknowledgements

UKTV History would like to thank Lion Television for
producing the TV series, *Britain's Best*.